Edward and Joan Redmayne

Basic English

MACMILLAN

Contents

1 **The Alphabet** capital letters, vowels and consonants, alphabetical order, using dictionaries 4
2 **Common Nouns** definition and examples 6
3 **Verbs** definition, active and passive verbs, verbs and nouns 8
4 **Adjectives** definition, numbers as adjectives 10
5 **Tenses** definition, past, present and future tenses 12
6 **Adverbs** definition, 'how, when and where', adverbial phrases 14
7 **Gender** masculine, feminine, common and neuter 16
Checkpoints 18
8 **Pronouns** definition, possessive pronouns 20
9 **Singular and Plural** definition, how to form plurals from different word endings 22
10 **Conjunctions** definition and examples 24
11 **Proper Nouns** definition and examples 26
12 **Related Words** definition and examples 28
13 **Link Words** who, which, that, whom 30
14 **Prepositions** definition, examples 32
Checkpoints 34
15 **Sentences** capital letters, use of punctuation, use in context 36
16 **Spelling** letters and sounds 38
17 **Apostrophes** in shortened words, definition, examples, *it's* and *its* 40
18 **Apostrophes** showing possession, examples 42
19 **Comparing Adjectives** definition and examples 44
20 **Collective Nouns** definition and examples 46
21 **Abstract Nouns** definition and examples 47
Checkpoints 48
22 **Speaking and Writing** use of question marks and inverted commas, position of inverted commas in writing speech, use of capital letters in writing speech 50
23 **Spelling Guide** practical guide to some of the rules of spelling, and exceptions to the rules 52
24 **More Spelling** 'i before e except after c' and silent letters 54
25 **Test Your Spelling** 56
26 **Idioms** definition and examples 58
27 **Capital Letters** summary of use 60
28 **Opposites** using different words, prefixes and suffixes to make words of opposite meaning 62
Checkpoints 64

29 **Similar Words** words similar in meaning to each other   66
30 **Building Words** using prefixes and suffixes   68
31 **Comparative Adverbs** definition and examples   70
32 **Similes** definition and examples   72
33 **Time Conjunctions** definition and examples   74
34 **Metaphors** definition and examples   76
   Checkpoints   78
35 **Homonyms** definition and examples   80
36 **Meaning and Emphasis** how to use words and sounds to emphasise a piece of writing   82
37 **Making New Verbs** adding words to common verbs   84
38 **Abbreviations** definition and examples   86
39 **Contractions** examples   87
40 **Word Building** compound words, combining words   88
41 **Nouns as Adjectives** examples   90
42 **Slang** use in everyday speech   91
43 **Overworked Words** finding alternatives to common words   92
44 **Homophones** definition and examples   94
   Checkpoints   96
45 **Proverbs** definition and examples   98
46 **Thesaurus** a catalogue of associated words, how to use   100
47 **Where to Look** where to go to find information   102
   Last Checkpoints   104
   Reference Section   106
   Gender   107
   Collective Nouns   109
   Idioms   110
   Opposites   112
   Synonyms   114
   Prefixes   115
   Suffixes   116
   Similes   117
   Homonyms   118
   New Verbs Made by Adding Adverbs   119
   Abbreviations   120
   Compound Words   122
   Combining Words   123
   Homophones   124
   Proverbs   125
   Index   126
   Acknowledgements   128

1 The Alphabet

There are 26 letters in the alphabet. Each letter can be written in small letters (a,b,c,d,e,) or CAPITAL LETTERS (A,B,C,D,E).

Vowels and Consonants

Five letters are **vowels:** Aa Ee Ii Oo Uu. Capital I does *not* have a dot on it. Every English word contains at least one vowel. Sometimes 'y' is used as a vowel, in words like my, why, try, by and fly.
All the other letters are **consonants.**
Two letters are used as words on their own: I and A a. The word 'I' is *always* a capital letter.

    I like chips.   Who am I?   Here I am.

Why do you say: *an* apple, *an* old man, *an* unmarried woman?

Alphabetical Order

Many lists, such as dictionaries, registers, telephone directories and address books, are in alphabetical order. This makes it easy to find words and names in the list.

1 A dictionary begins with all the words starting with the letter **A**. Then follow all those starting with **B**, then **C**, and so on through the alphabet.

2 Words starting with the same letter are sorted by the alphabetical order of the second letter:

    b<u>a</u>t comes before b<u>o</u>at   m<u>o</u>re comes before m<u>u</u>ddle

3 Where groups of words start with the same letters, they are in order of the *next* letter of each word:

    bot<u>t</u>le comes before bo<u>w</u>l   crum<u>b</u> comes before cru<u>s</u>h
    thro<u>a</u>t comes before thro<u>u</u>gh

Finding Words

At the top of each page in a dictionary there are two words in heavy black letters. These are **index words**, and are the first and last words on the page. Index words help you to find where the word is.

Starters

Say the alphabet. Say it from **G** onwards. Say it from **M** onwards. Say it from **R** onwards.

Written Practice

1 Arrange each group of words in alphabetical order:
    a. bread rake lean sand arch
    b. pen nail rest orange quiet
    c. zebra jump catch island dove

2 Write down the names of five of your friends in alphabetical order.

3 Put each set of words in alphabetical order:
    a. mean more man mist must
    b. stretch stone style stain stun
    c. throttle throne throat through throb

Dictionary Practice

In your dictionary, find these words and write out their meanings:
    a. museum mammoth moderate meddle marsupial
    b. summit sympathy safari search seldom

2 Common Nouns

The *Mole* had been working very hard all the *morning*, spring-cleaning his little *home*. First with *brooms*, then with *dusters*; then on *ladders* and *steps* and *chairs*, with a *brush* and a *pail* of *whitewash*; till he had *dust* in his *throat* and *eyes*, and *splashes* of *whitewash* all over his black *fur*, and an aching *back* and weary *arms*.
(from The Wind in the Willows by Kenneth Grahame)

All the words in italics are **nouns**. Nouns name things.
A noun often answers the question, 'What is that?'

    It is a *house*.   It is a *cat*.   This is a *bud*.
    That is a *wall*.   It is a *fly*.   This is a *leaf*.
    Here is a *door*.   It is a *robin*.   This is a *flower*.
    It is a *window*.   It is a *kangaroo*.   This is a *twig*.

All the words in italics are nouns. Nouns are names for people, places and things.

In Section 22 you will learn about **abstract nouns** – names of feelings and ideas.

Starters

1 Name five things smaller than a matchbox.
2 Think of ten nouns that are living things.
3 Pick out the nouns mentioned in this song.

    Oh! the dust on the feather,
    And the feather on the bird,
    And the bird on the eggs,
    And the eggs in the nest,
    And the nest on the branch,
    And the branch on the tree,
    And the tree in the ground,
    And the green grass grew all round . . .

Written Practice

The answer to each question is a noun.

1 What is the name of buildings where:
   films are shown   goods are made   cars are kept
   things are sold   meals are served   horses are kept
   money is looked after   books are borrowed

2 What are the nouns that name someone who:
   treats sick people   rides horses in races
   writes for a newspaper   sells flowers
   investigates crime   studies the stars
   takes bets   flies an aeroplane
   plans buildings

3 What is the name of:
   a hot, sandy, waste land   the home of a hare
   a lorry which carries oil   a fox's home
   a beaver's home   an otter's home
   a van which takes sick people to hospital
   something which measures temperature

Free for All

1 The words 'game' and 'sport' are nouns. Make a list of as many games and sports as you can.

2 Choose one of the nouns below. Then write down other nouns that have something to do with the one you choose.
   street   house   sea   space
Begin like this: street – pavement, traffic, pedestrian . . .

3 Verbs

What are these people doing?

Verbs answer the questions:

What are you doing?	What did you do?	What are you going to do?
I am walking	I was thinking	I shall stay
I jump	I guessed	I shall refuse
I am playing	I was talking	I will go
I write	I wished	I shall try

Some of these verbs are actions: *to walk, to jump, to talk.*
Some of them are not actions, but are still verbs: *to wish, to try.*
Think of other verbs like these.

Active and Passive Verbs

You can use verbs in two ways.

The first way is **active**: *The cat ate the mouse.*

But you could write this sentence the other way round: *The mouse was eaten by the cat.*

Or you need not say who did it at all: *The mouse was eaten.*

These are **passive**.

Active	Passive
The bus hit me.	I was hit by a bus.
A dog bit Tom's ankle.	Tom's ankle was bitten by a dog.
My mother makes the cakes.	The cakes are made by my mother.

8

Verbs and Nouns

Sometimes words can be used as verbs *or* nouns.

    Verb   *Noun*
    I *hurry*.   I am in a *hurry*.
    I am *walking*.   I am going for a *walk*.
    I am *swimming*. *Swimming* is fun.

Can you think of other words like this?

Starters

1 Think of some verbs you can mime. Then ask your partner which verb you are miming. Here are two ideas:
    I am sawing.   I am throwing.
2 Look around and write down the things which you can see people doing:
    She is sitting.   He is writing . . .

Written Practice

1 Write these sentences in the passive.
    a. A crowd of people saw the landslide.
    b. Arsenal won the football match.
    c. A dog bit my brother.
    d. A clever thief stole the diamonds.
    e. A policeman took the lost boy home.

2 Write these sentences in the active.
    a. It was lost by my father.
    b. The stone was thrown by John Jones.
    c. A tree was planted by the prince.
    d. The dinner was cooked by their mother.
    e. The prizes were presented by the Lord Mayor.

Free for All

Think of all the things you can do with your body. Write down each movement you can make:
    I am wriggling my toes.   I am clenching my fist . . .

4 Adjectives

Adjectives help to tell you more about nouns. You use adjectives to describe things, people, animals and places.

a *thick* rope   a *thin* man   a *fierce* lion   a *busy* street

Describe the dog:
    It is a *savage* dog.
    It is a *Scottish* dog.
    It is a *noisy* dog.
    It is a *black* dog.
    It is a *small* dog.

How would you describe your friend?
    He is *shy*.   She is *talkative*.
    He is *quiet*.   She is *mischievous*.
    He is *kind*.   She is *cheerful*.
    He is *clever*.   She is *untidy*.

All these words are adjectives.

Numbers

Numbers are adjectives. They tell you 'how many':
> *one* partridge in a pear tree   *five* fingers on a hand   *eleven* footballers in a team   *twelve* months in a year   *three hundred and sixty-six* days in a leap year

Some adjectives tell you how many, but not the *exact* number:
> *all* the footballers   *many* shots   *several* players   *some* fouls   *few* goals

Whose Is It?

Some adjectives are used to say who owns something:
> *my* hat; *your* coat; *his* bicycle; *her* comb; *its* beak; *our* friends; *their* uncle.

Written Practice

1 Write out these adjectives with suitable nouns

black	curly	patient	energetic
agile	smooth	angry	calm
narrow	sharp	kind	dangerous
delicate	red	deceitful	exciting
tasty	three	honest	sad

2 Match the adjectives in the first list with the nouns from the second list:

English   Scottish   American   German   Spanish

onion   sausage   dollar   bagpipe   Channel

3 Choose the right number to complete the phrases below. Write each number in words:
> ____ days in a week   ____ toes on my feet
> ____ sides of a square   ____ wheels on a bicycle

Free for All

Write three sentences to describe your best friend. Underline the adjectives you use.

5 Tenses

The **tense** of a verb tells **when** the action takes place.

Past	Present	Future
earlier today	now	later today
yesterday	at this moment	tomorrow
last week		next week
last month		next month
last year		next year
long ago		in the 21st century

Past tense	Present tense	Future tense
I was	I am	I will be
I had	I have	I will have
I was having	I am having	I shall have
You did	You do	You will do
You were doing	You are doing	
He went	He goes	He will go
He was going	He is going	
It happened	It happens	It will happen
It was happening	It is happening	
We wrote	We write	We will write
We were writing	We are writing	We shall write
They tried	They try	They will try
They were trying	They are trying	

Starters

Say whether each of the following is in the present, past or future:

yesterday	tomorrow	when I was a baby
today	next week	the present time
now	last century	the day after tomorrow
my next birthday	a fortnight ago	on my 21st birthday
in the year 2000	this minute	the day before yesterday

Written Practice

1 Change the following into the past tense:
    a. I am eating a boiled egg.
    b. I begin to understand.
    c. The field is full of black and white cows.
    d. I feel like jumping over the moon.
    e. The cat creeps along the grass towards the frog.
    f. I hate going to the dentist.

2 Write sentences beginning with the words below. Underline all the verbs you use.
    a. Last night . . .
    b. Soon . . .
    c. At this moment . . .
    d. I remember . . .
    e. During the last holiday . . .

Free for All

1 It is fairly easy to write in the past tense. You write about something that has happened. Use the past tense and write a diary for yesterday.
2 Writing in the present tense is harder. Use the present tense and write what you can see taking place *now*.
3 Use the future tense and write a short story called 'When I am 21'.

6 Adverbs

Slowly
Slowly the tide creeps up the sand.
Slowly the shadows cross the land.
Slowly the cart horse pulls his mile.
Slowly the old man mounts the stile.
Slowly the hands move round the clock.
Slowly the dew dries on the dock.
Slow is the snail – but slowest of all
The green moss spreads on the old brick wall.
(From *Wandering Moon* by James Reeves)

In this poem the poet tells *how* different things move.

1. These adverbs tell **how** an action is done.
    He walked *quickly*.   He stood *still*.   She spoke *truthfully*.
    He sat *upright*.   She tried *hard*.   She thought *carefully*.

2. Some adverbs tell **when** an action is done.
    Dan arrived *early*.   I will go *soon*.
    She answered *immediately*.   The holidays start *tomorrow*.
    Simon is working *now*.   Jane came home *yesterday*.

3. These adverbs tell **where** an action takes place.
    David stopped *here*.   Ann went *away*.
    She placed it *there*.   He stayed *outside*.

Very often you use a phrase to tell how, when or where an action is done.
These phrases are called **adverbial phrases**.
Read across:
   He arrived *early*.   He arrived *at exactly one o'clock*.
   I will go *soon*.   I will go *a week on Tuesday*.
   She returned *immediately*.   She returned *very late at night*.

Simon stopped *here*. Simon stopped *by the school gate*.
She placed it *there*. She placed it *on the table*.
The car skidded *sideways*. The car skidded *into the ditch*.
She sang *sweetly*. He sang *in a husky voice*.

Starters

1 Think of adverbs which tell how these actions are done?
   I ran ____   He fought ____   She struggled ____
   It moved ____   She smiled ____   He whispered ____
   I shouted ____   It climbed ____   He fell ____
2 Say when and where these actions happened:
   Yesterday I fell *in the river*.
   ____ I walked ____
   ____ we had lunch ____
   ____ the car lurched ____
   ____ I threw the ball ____

Written Practice

1 Write out these sentences using one adverb instead of the adverbial phrases underlined.
   a. The scientist worked <u>with great care.</u>
   b. She spoke <u>in a soft voice.</u>
   c. He tripped and fell <u>on the ground.</u>
   d. The salesman talked <u>without stopping.</u>

2 You can do all these things:
   run walk crawl climb play
But how do you do them? Some of these adverbs may give you ideas:
   swiftly slowly with jerky steps clumsily with great enthusiasm
Write 5 sentences using the verbs above with adverbs or adverbial phrases which tell of your own movements.

7 Gender

Masculine and Feminine

To find the gender of a noun you ask the question, 'Is it male or female?' Sometimes there are different words for the male and female. Here are some nouns giving the masculine and feminine gender of people:

Masculine	Feminine
He is a *man*.	*She* is a *woman*.
He is my *brother*.	*She* is my *sister*.
He is my *uncle*.	*She* is my *aunt*.
He is an *actor*.	*She* is an *actress*.
He is a *king*.	*She* is a *queen*.

(Notice the pronouns *he* and *she* are masculine and feminine too.)

Different nouns are often used to name male and female animals:

dog and bitch   stallion and mare
bull and cow   drake and duck

Common Gender

Sometimes the same words are used for both the male and female:

baby   animal   child
friend   bird   frog
teenager   visitor   whale

Neuter Gender

Many nouns are names of things which are without life or sex.

Up the *road* there is a *house* made of *stone* and *brick* and thatched with *straw*.
In my *desk* I have a *pen*, a *pencil*, a *ruler*, a *book*, and a *ball*.
The foods I like are *chips, sausages, eggs, bread, jam* and *biscuits*.

Some people talk of lifeless things as *she*.

"She's a fine ship," said the sailor.
"She's a reliable old car," said its owner.

Sometimes we refer to living things as *it*.
>It's an old dog.   It's a clean cat.
>It's a lively old horse.   It's a beautiful baby.

Starters

Are you male or female?
Think of ten nouns for people of your sex. Begin:
>headmaster, uncle, . . . **or** headmistress, aunt, . . .

Written Practice

1 Write these sentences, changing the gender of the words underlined:
>My <u>mother</u> met me.   <u>She</u> was with my <u>aunt</u>.
>I have one <u>brother</u>.   His <u>father</u> is a <u>waiter</u>.
>I like <u>her</u>.   <u>Her sister</u> married my <u>brother</u>.

2 Make two lists headed *Masculine* and *Feminine*. Write each of the following in the correct column:
>daughter king monk wife billy-goat vixen sow stag heifer prince widower wizard pea-hen bullock gander filly witch bridegroom

3 Give the opposite gender of:
>gentleman lass him Mr lioness goose duchess mayor hostess bachelor heir male bride

4 Many occupations have different words for male and female workers. How many can you think of? Here are two to start you off:
>actor, actress, . . .

Can you think of twenty nouns of common gender? Begin:
>walker, writer . . .

Checkpoints

A

1. Write ten common nouns beginning with the letter 'm'.
2. Pick out the verbs in these sentences.
    a. He ran home.
    b. My father gave me £1.
    c. She turned and smiled.
    d. Stop and think before you begin.
    e. She fell from her horse, rolled a few yards, then lay still.
3. Which three letters follow immediately after:
    q   i   t   m   w
4. Write ten nouns which are the names of:
    a. flowers or trees   b. vehicles   c. tools
5. Write these sentences in the past tense:
    I am going home. My sister will come with me. Mother will be waiting for us.
6. Write sentences using each of these verbs as a noun:
    walk   ride   dream   try   taste
7. Write the nouns of common gender which mean a person who:
    a. takes part in a game   e. travels by bus or train
    b. is ill in hospital   f. travels on foot
    c. collects   g. makes speeches
    d. swims   h. goes to school
8. Pick out the verb, adverbs, nouns and adjectives:
    The faithful dog walked obediently beside its ageing master.

B

1. Change the gender of each noun in these sentences:
    a. The waiter served the lady and then the gentleman.
    b. I went out with my father and uncle and my sister stayed with my mother and aunt.
2. Arrange these sets of words in alphabetical order:
    a. oak beech ash sycamore yew
    b. indistinct inflate incident insurance incomplete
    c. drown drum drone drizzle drop
    d. straw strap strain straight stray
3. What is the common noun which is the name of the person who:
    a. looks after sheep
    b. operates on people in hospital
    c. studies the past
    d. looks after people's eyes
    e. works underground getting coal, gold or precious stones
4. Pick out the adverbs from these sentences:
    a. He entered the room slowly. He searched carefully and soon found what he was looking for.
    b. Please stop now and put your books in your desk.
5. Write these sentences in the present tense:
    I walked to school and traffic roared past. At the crossing I crossed safely.

8 Pronouns

Pronouns stand for nouns. They are short words. Here are the main ones:

    I   you he   she it we   you they
    me you him her it us   you them

Imagine your name was Pat Smith and you asked your mother for 20p. This is what would happen if there were no pronouns.

Pat Smith went hopefully to Pat Smith's mother. After a few moments, Pat Smith asked Pat Smith's mother if Pat Smith's mother would give Pat Smith 20p. Pat Smith's mother sighed, found Pat Smith's mother's purse, opened Pat Smith's mother's purse, and gave 20p to Pat Smith.

Here it is with pronouns.

I went hopefully to mother and after a few moments asked *her* if *she* would give *me* 20p. *She* sighed, found *her* purse, opened *it* and gave *me* 20p.

Some pronouns are used to show who owns something. They are called **possessive pronouns**.

    mine yours his hers ours theirs

Examples:

    That hat is *yours*. This one is *mine*.
    These books are in a muddle. Which are *his* and which are *hers*?
    The red cards are *yours*, the green ones are *theirs* and the blue ones are *ours*.

Double pronouns. You often use two pronouns together.

    You and *I* came home.   Pat spoke to *you* and *me*.

Notice that double pronouns are used together in one sentence instead of using two separate sentences.

You came home.   *I* came home.   *You* and *I* came home.
Pat spoke to *you*.   Pat spoke to *me*.   Pat spoke to *you* and *me*.

Starters

In the following sentences, which nouns do the underlined pronouns refer to?
1 Dad carried the bottle to the kitchen. At the sink <u>he</u> dropped <u>it</u>.
2 My mother bought some sweets and <u>she</u> gave <u>them</u> to me.
3 When the dog saw its master <u>it</u> turned and followed <u>him</u>.
4 Joan and Rex struggled up the slope. <u>She</u> slipped but held on to <u>him</u>.
5 The little child ran away from its parents and fell over. We picked <u>it</u> up and took <u>it</u> back to <u>them</u>.
6 These flowers are from my sister. <u>She</u> told me to give <u>them</u> to you.

Written Practice

1 Write four sentences about yourself using the pronouns *I*, *me*, and *mine*.

2 Rewrite this passage using pronouns:
Steve and Cindy decided to go for a ride in the car. Steve got the car out of the garage, started the car and Steve and Cindy set off. The car went fine at first then the car conked out. Steve could not get the car going again, so Steve pushed the car and Cindy steered the car. Steve and Cindy were fed up. Cindy said, "Sell that car and buy a new car."

3 Write these sentences again but use nouns instead of the pronouns underlined:
<u>He</u> threw <u>it</u>.   <u>It</u> barked at <u>him</u>.   <u>We</u> like <u>them</u>.

4 Use *you* and *I* or *you* and *me* to complete these sentences
   a. – and – are invited to the party.
   b. John will stay but – and – must leave.
   c. He will send for – and – later.
   d. There is room for – and – in the car.
   e. Soon – and – will meet again.

9 Singular and Plural

Singular means one.   **Plural** means more than one.
Pick out the plurals in this passage:

> There were more strangers walking about the village: stranded train passengers in town clothes, ladies in mink, gentlemen in fur-lined overcoats. There were a great many soldiers and volunteers.
>
> (from *Avalanche* by A. Rutgers van der Loeff)

How to Form Plurals

For most plurals add an 's' to the singular:
>sticks apes tins gifts papers birds pavements bicycles

For words ending in ch, sh, ss, x, (hissing sounds), add 'es':
>ditches matches rushes dishes dresses classes boxes waxes

For words ending in -ay, -ey, -oy, add 's':
>ways days keys donkeys monkeys chimneys boys toys

For other words ending in y, change the y to 'ies':
>cities countries ladies babies tries flies difficulties berries

For some words ending in -f, add 's':
>dwarfs roofs chiefs cliffs whiffs

For other words ending in -f, change the f to 'ves':
>halves calves leaves knives wives loaves thieves

For words ending in -o, add 'es':
>heroes tomatoes potatoes negroes

Learn these exceptions: pianos solos

Some words do not change at all: sheep deer cod salmon scissors swine

In some words only the vowel(s) changes: man – men   foot – feet

Starters

1 Without looking, can you remember the rules for making the plurals of:
>tomato donkey cliff pass leaf goose

2 Give the plurals of the following:

puff	domino	patch	mouse	half	boss
party	knife	place	ferry	piano	scarf
woman	fly	church	lady	echo	difficulty

3 Give the singulars of:

potatoes	keys	lives	thieves
tries	fishes	loaves	friends
princesses	babies	trips	stories
passers-by	families		

Written Practice

1 Complete these lists. Start like this:

a book	two books	one –	six pies
the –	many boats	a spy	two –
a torch	three –	a –	many buses
one shelf	several –	one calf	two –
a tray	four –	a fox	four –

2 Write the plurals of:

			city	berry
country	roof	chief	trousers	wolf
elf	wife	penny	penalty	lioness
goose	mouse	salmon		

3 Write the plural nouns which are:
   a. the foliage of trees and plants
   b. insects with beautifully coloured wings
   c. small time-pieces worn on the wrist
   d. used for biting
   e. married women
   f. new-born cows

4 Make three columns as below and write down as many examples of each type of noun as you can:

Nouns ending in -ch, -sh, -ss and -x with -es plural	Nouns ending in -y with -ies plural	Nouns ending in -f or -fe with -ves plural
hutch hutches	family families	leaf leaves

10 Conjunctions

The words <u>and</u>, <u>but</u>, <u>either</u>, <u>or</u>, <u>neither</u>, <u>nor</u> are joining words. They are called **conjunctions**. They are used to join other words and parts of sentences together.

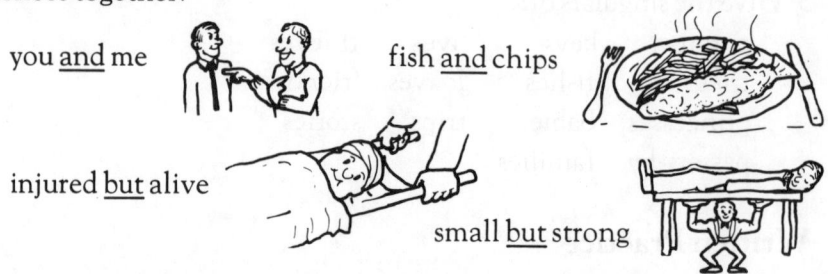

you <u>and</u> me

fish <u>and</u> chips

injured <u>but</u> alive

small <u>but</u> strong

a. I hate tapioca <u>but</u> I like semolina.
b. Granny wouldn't look after Tabby <u>as</u> she didn't like cats.
c. Jean was thin <u>because</u> she didn't eat much.
d. Hugh's bicycle had disappeared <u>so</u> he went to the police.
e. Mother bought us all an ice cream <u>although</u> she didn't have much money.
f. The dog will be punished <u>unless</u> he starts behaving better.
g. Ask the conductor <u>if</u> this bus is going to Archway.
h. The doctor climbed into his new red car <u>and</u> drove off at high speed.
i. <u>Either</u> go outside and play football <u>or</u> help me wash up.
j. <u>Both</u> the roof <u>and</u> the chimney were damaged in the storm.

All the underlined words are conjunctions.

Starters

1 Think of ten pairs of things and people that are often joined together with 'and'. Begin:
    bread <u>and</u> butter   Jack <u>and</u> Jill
2 Think of six phrases using 'but' to join two different ideas:
    slow <u>but</u> sure   dangerous <u>but</u> exciting

Written Practice

1 Make sentences using the following conjunctions:
   Both ... and   Either ... or
   Neither ... nor

2 Use a suitable conjunction to complete each of these sentences:
   a. I wanted to go to the fair ... I hadn't any money.
   b. The teacher was cross ... Peter hadn't been listening.
   c. ... John ... his sister could swim.
   d. Dad said I couldn't watch television ... I had finished my homework.
   e. David did the washing-up ... I did the drying.

3 Some people use 'and' too much. Read this passage:
   I ran away like a shot and out of the corner of my eye I could see the big fellow chasing me and he was shouting and swearing at me and I put on a spurt and jumped a low fence and then I dodged round the corner of a warehouse and ran inside and jumped into an old packing case and covered myself with straw.

   It's not very good, is it?
   Write out the story in sentences. Don't use 'and' so often but try to make the story lively and interesting.

11 Proper Nouns

Charles Dickens was born on 7 February 1812 at Landport, near Portsmouth, England. His father, John Dickens, was a clerk in the Naval Pay Office and his grandparents had been in service to Lord Crewe. Charles became a journalist, and went to America in 1842 and 1867–8 and to Italy in 1844. He died at his Gad's Hill home in Kent on 9 June 1870.

You use **proper nouns** to name people, places, days and months. Each proper noun begins with a capital letter. Pick out all the proper nouns in the passage above.

My name is <u>Robert</u>.
I live in <u>London</u>.
Her name is <u>Joan Smith</u>.
She lives in <u>Elm Park Mansions</u>.
This is <u>Waterloo</u> station.
Thirty days have <u>September</u>,
<u>April</u>, <u>June</u> and <u>November</u>.

<u>Solomon Grundy</u>,
Born on <u>Monday</u>,
Christened on <u>Tuesday</u>,
Married on <u>Wednesday</u>,
Took ill on <u>Thursday</u>,
Worse on <u>Friday</u>,
Died on <u>Saturday</u>,
Buried on <u>Sunday</u>.

All the underlined words are proper nouns.

Starters

1 Go through the alphabet and think of one boy's and one girl's name beginning with each letter.
2 Name six towns. Start with the town you live in.

Written Practice

1 Which country is associated with each of the following?
Each answer is a proper noun and should begin with a capital letter.

    kilts   frogs' legs   bulb fields
    bull fighting chopsticks   tea
    kangaroos   watches   cowboys

2 a. What are the first names of two people in your family?
    b. Which countries make up the United Kingdom?
    c. Which book contains the Old Testament and the New Testament?
    d. Which ocean is between Europe and America?
    e. Which programme do you like best on television?

3 Write in full the words which have the first letter missing:
    a. My friends' names are __ohn and __hristopher.
    b. __he last month of the year follows __ovember.
    c. __ondon is the capital of the __nited __ingdom.
    d. __he highest mountain in the world is __ount __verest.
    e. __ast week I read the book __*reasure* __*sland* by __obert __ouis __tevenson.

4 a. Which days of the week have six letters?
    b. Which day of the week has a silent letter?
    c. If today is Tuesday, what was the day before yesterday?
    d. Which days do we say are 'the weekend'?
    e. If yesterday was Wednesday, what will be the day after tomorrow?
    f. Which month of the year has only three letters?
    g. Write the 9th, the 6th and the 2nd months of the year.

Free for All

On a map find:
    a. the five continents
    b. five European countries
    c. five African countries
    d. five rivers
    e. five seas or oceans
    f. five mountains

12 Related Words

I'll get you a job, Giraffe!
Do you hear?
We shall build buildings together!
(from 'To a Giraffe' by Patricia Hubbell)

In the poem, 'buildings' comes from 'build'. They are different forms of the same word. Many nouns have adjectives and verbs related to them. For example:
1. Noun: action – It was a brave *action*.
   Adjective: active – She is an *active* member of the class.
   Verb: act – Think before you *act*.
2. Noun: Can you guess the *width* of the river?
   Adjective: He has *wide* shoulders.
   Verb: The river begins to *widen* here.
3. Noun: The baby is a *joy* to its parents.
   Adjective: The winner was in a *joyful* mood.
   Verb: Did you *enjoy* it?
4. Noun: There was *confusion* in the room when the lights went out.
   Adjective: This is a very *confused* plan.
   Verb: Do not *confuse* 'stationary' and 'stationery'.

Starters

1. Make adjectives from these nouns:
   obedience   pity   success   warmth   width
   thought   poison   moisture   reality   loss
2. Make nouns from these adjectives:
   sensible   friendly   deceitful   beautiful   free
   hateful   forceful   grassy   grievous   equal
3. Make verbs from these nouns:
   description   belief   choice   recognition   width
   punishment   ascent   thought   variety   peace

Written Practice

1 Make three columns and complete each set of related words:

Noun	Adjective	Verb
amusement	amusing	amuse
___	descriptive	___
exhaustion	___	___
___	inventive	___
___	___	obey
laziness	___	___
___	knowledgeable	___

2 Write sentences using each of these words:
   a. danger   dangerous   endanger
   b. length   long   lengthen
   c. life   alive   live

3 Sometimes the same word can be used as two different parts of speech.
   Noun: I haven't a *care* in the world.
   Verb: I don't *care* about games.

Here are some others: plan poison free pity fight walk
Can you think of any more? Write sentences using:
   a. poison as a verb
   b. free as an adjective
   c. fight as a noun
   d. walk as a noun
   e. fight as a verb
   f. plan as a verb

13 Link Words: Who, Which, That, Whom

You often use the words **who**, **which**, **that** and **whom** to link two sentences.

There is the boy. He won the prize.
There is the boy *who* won the prize.
We have a cat. It catches mice.
We have a cat *which* catches mice.
I saw the children and parcels. They filled the car.
I saw the children and parcels *that* filled the car.
I met a man. I knew him.
I met a man *whom* I knew.

Use *who* and *whom* for people.
Use *which* for things.
Use *that* for people or things.

Who   Was it Tom who found the money?
Which   The lion, which escaped from its cage, savaged the keeper.
That   He is the greatest man that ever lived.
          It was the highest cliff that anyone had seen.
Whom   A friend to whom I was speaking told me about it.
          The person by whom you were sitting is my sister.

Starters

1 Use *who*, *which*, *that* or *whom* to join each pair of these sentences:
    a. I like the picture. It hangs in my bedroom.
    b. Pam recognised the actor. He had appeared on television.
    c. We saw the passengers and their cases. They filled the coach.
    d. Mavis is a kind person. I admire her very much.

2 Who or what does the word underlined refer to in these sentences?
    a. I know the girl who won the prize.
    b. People who live in glass houses shouldn't throw stones.
    c. There is the dog that bit the milkman.

Written Practice

1 Write out and complete these sentences by using *who*, *which*, *that* or *whom*:
    a. Here is the sparrow ____ killed Cock Robin.
    b. We will follow the road ____ leads to the castle.
    c. The man ____ I helped was blind.
    d. The book ____ I put on the desk has disappeared.
    e. I saw the plane ____ crashed.

2 Complete these sentences by using *to whom*, *from whom*, *by whom* or *which*:
    a. There is the girl ____ you borrowed the book.
    b. The puzzle ____ I solved baffled my father.
    c. I am the person ____ you owe the money.

3 Choose the right word or words from the brackets:
    a. All those (who, that, which) like football, stand up.
    b. The soldiers (which, whom, who) had been betrayed were led away to death.
    c. I trod on the cat (whom, which, that) was sitting on the mat.
    d. The man (whom, who, to whom) I offered a drink smiled at me.
    e. (By whom, From whom, Which) have you brought this message?

Free for All

Complete these sentences:
    a. The girl who ____
    b. The horse which ____
    c. The desk that ____
    d. The man to whom ____

14 Prepositions

You use a **preposition** before a noun. It connects the noun with the rest of the sentence.

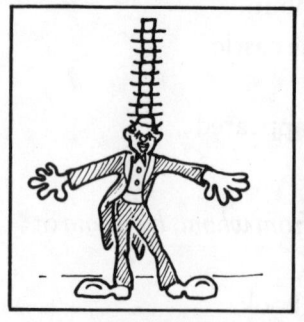

balanced <u>on</u> his head

jumped <u>over</u> the stream

leaned <u>against</u> the wall

fell <u>into</u> a ditch

The plane flew <u>above</u> the clouds.
Tim met his friend <u>at</u> the bus stop.
Susan sat <u>beside</u> Mary.
Mary sat <u>between</u> Susan and Lucy.
The dictionary is <u>on</u> the table.

He climbed <u>up</u> the hill.
The car crashed <u>through</u> the wall.
The coin rolled <u>down</u> a grid.
I walked <u>under</u> a ladder.
The man fell <u>off</u> the ladder.

All the words underlined are prepositions. Here are some others:

about	across	after	along	among	before
below	beyond	by	from	in	near
of	round	to	towards	until	with

Sometimes you use two prepositions together:
> I went down into the cellar.
> She ran away from the crowd.

Can you think of more?

Written Practice

1 Put each of these phrases in a sentence:
> in the street   by the window
> down a hole   at the supermarket

2 Choose the best preposition from the words in brackets to use in these sentences:
   a. He threw the ball (at, to, near) the wicket.
   b. The key was (into, until, in) the lock.
   c. Mum was pleased (at, with, to) my sister.
   d. The chocolates were (in, round) a box (over, on, at) the table.
   e. Smoke went (without, up, after) the chimney and (up, out of, over) the chimney pot.

3 Often you may use different prepositions to change the meaning of a sentence:
> The ball went *near* the window.
> The ball went *through* the window.

Now use at least two different prepositions with each sentence, to give each sentence at least two different meaning:
   a. The book was ____ the table.
   b. The burglar ran ____ the road.
   c. The post office is ____ the church.
   d. Brian found his book ____ a pile of rubbish.
   e. The ship sailed ____ the harbour.

Checkpoints

A

1 Rewrite these sentences using pronouns where suitable:
    a. John gave John's friend a birthday present.
    b. The teacher said the teacher wanted to speak to the two boys when the two boys came back to school.
    c. Pat looked at the anorak and said that the anorak was Pat's.

2 Write sentences giving: your full name, the town where you were born, the town you live in now, your country and continent.

3 Complete these sentences by using adjectives formed from these nouns:
    a. poverty: He is a ____ man and has very little money.
    b. energy: The games' teacher is lively and ____.
    c. spite: Many ____ things have been said about her.

4 Complete these sentences using *who*, *which* or *that* in the correct place:
    a. The dog ____ savaged a young child was put down.
    b. The first person ____ gets the answer wins.
    c. ____ can tell me ____ of the boxes is heavier?

5 Choose the right preposition to use in these sentences:
    a. The two girls divided the sweets ____ them.
    b. This pattern is different ____ that one.
    c. The sweets were shared equally ____ the three boys.

6 Re-write these sentences in the plural:
    a. The thief stole a loaf of bread and a box of biscuits.
    b. The lady rode the pony towards the stable.
    c. The child could not reach the blackberry on the high branch.

B

1 if   unless   because   although   whether

Complete the sentences with one of the conjunctions above:
- a. The old man could not decide ____ to go out or watch T.V.
- b. I will not go ____ you come with me.
- c. We are going for a picnic tomorrow ____ the weather is fine.
- d. Tom fell into the stream ____ he had been told not to go near it.
- e. I am going to meet Mary ____ I promised to.

2 Put these words in the plural:

knife half donkey shelf
chief pony box chimney

3 Which country does a person come from who is:

Dutch   Swiss   Danish French   Italian
Ghanaian American Irish   Norwegian English

4 Pick out the prepositions:
- a. Paul hid behind the curtain.
- b. John scrambled under the table.
- c. I had £2 in my purse.
- d. We walked slowly round the house and into the garden.

Write other sentences using each preposition.

5 Join these pairs of sentences using *who, which, whose, that* or *to whom*:
- a. We met a coastguard. He saved a girl from drowning.
- b. At the car park we saw the driver. His car had been stolen.
- c. In this stable is the horse. It has thrown its rider.
- d. Here is the boy. I lent my bicycle to him.

15 Sentences: Capital Letters, Full Stops and Commas

I held out my hand, and the horrible, soft-spoken, eyeless creature gripped it in a moment like a vice. I was so much startled that I struggled to withdraw; but the blind man pulled me close up to him with a single action of his arm. "Now, boy," he said, "take me in to the captain."

(from *Treasure Island* by R. L. Stevenson)

Writing in sentences makes what you write easy to read and understand. A sentence begins with a capital letter and ends with a full stop, question mark or exclamation mark. This is the punctuation you use to separate one sentence from others round it. It also makes your meaning clear. Read these words:

    I told you yesterday you would not believe me

Now read them again and notice the difference that punctuation makes:

    I told you yesterday. You would not believe me.

    I told you. Yesterday you would not believe me.

But sentences must make sense when you read them together. They must link what comes before with what follows.

Here is a sentence: *Joe turned away.*

That means very little on its own, but it means much more when you read it now:

> *A small crowd had gathered at the edge of the pavement. Joe pushed forward, curious to see what it was about. Then he saw. Dan's black and white dog was lying in the gutter! Joe turned away. How could he tell his friend that his dog was dead?*

Pauses   The *full stop* is the longest pause and it helps you to understand what you read. The *comma* is the shortest pause. Read these sentences and pause at each comma. Notice how it helps to make the meaning clear.

    Mother bought bread, butter, bacon and cheese.

Notice a comma is *not* placed before 'and'

    The man was old, wrinkled and toothless.

    Pam, who was very nervous, never said a word.

Starters

1 In one sentence, name four things that you can see. Begin:
   From where I am sitting I can see ____
2 Write out two questions you would ask someone whom you had not met before.

Written Practice

1 Write these jumbled proverbs in sentences:
   a. before you look leap
   b. hot the iron while is strike
   c. no stone gathers a rolling moss
   d. is a hand bird in the worth the bush in two
   e. many broth spoil the too cooks

2 Re-arrange these words and write them as sentences:
   a. ends stop with a full sentence a
   b. the dog the stranger barked at
   c. birthday made a mother cake
   d. the landing aircraft crashed on
   e. every capital letter begins with a sentence

3 Write out these sentences with commas in the correct places:
   a. I can recognise sparrows thrushes blackbirds and seagulls.
   b. My friend is tall fair bright and cheerful.
   c. The dog stood stiff-legged bared its teeth snarled snapped and then lunged to attack.
   d. My sister who likes flowers bought some seeds yesterday.
   e. Two boys who were in Class 4 started the trouble.

4 Arrange these sentences in the right order and then write them out.
   Begin: Our car ____
   a. A great cloud of steam rose and Father slammed the bonnet down again.
   b. Father got out and lifted the bonnet.
   c. Our car stopped with a loud hissing sound.
   d. "I hope it won't take long," said Mother.
   e. He got back into the car and said, "We'll wait until it cools down."

16 Spelling: Letters and Sounds

They turned the hissy-snake the other way round for the Z-sound, to show it was hissing backwards in a soft and gentle way; and they just made a twiddle for E, because it came into the picture so often; and so on and so forth and so following till they had done and drawn all the sound-pictures that they wanted, and there was the Alphabet, all complete.
(from *How the Alphabet Was Made* by Rudyard Kipling)

Go through the alphabet and say the sound of each letter.
As you sound each letter write a word which has the letter in it.
   Begin: able _____
Think carefully, because vowels have more than one sound:
   mad made   her here   pin pine
   hop hope   cut cute

Sound Patterns

Sometimes several letters combine to make one sound. They make a pattern that you can recognise. Read these words and say the sound of the letters in italics.

walk*er*	start*ing*	sta*tion*	inva*sion*
remind*er*	cry*ing*	posi*tion*	divi*sion*
help*er*	jok*ing*	men*tion*	confu*sion*
jump*er*	giggl*ing*	infla*tion*	persua*sion*

mis*sion*	cur*ious*	l*ight*	pati*ence*
pen*sion*	fur*ious*	f*ight*	lic*ence*
ten*sion*	env*ious*	h*eight*	sci*ence*
proces*sion*	industr*ious*	m*ight*	conveni*ence*

| ac*tive* | selec*tive* | prob*able* | miser*able* |
| talka*tive* | imagina*tive* | consider*able* | eat*able* |

Some words begin with a group of letters which make one sound. Read these words and say the sound of the letters in italics:

*st*reet	*thr*ee	*spl*ash	*wh*at	*sch*ool
*st*range	*thr*ift	*spl*endid	*wh*ere	*sch*eme
*st*rong	*thr*oat	*spl*inter	*wh*en	*sch*ooner
*st*retch	*thr*ough	*spl*utter	*wh*eel	*sch*olar

Starters

Write two other words which end with each of these groups of letters:

    -ious   -ight   -able   -ent   -tion

Written practice

1 Write three words which begin with each of these letters:

    sp____   tre____   sho____   th____   wh____

2 Write three words beginning with each of these prefixes:

    un____   in____   dis____   pre____   con____

    mis____

3 Say these words and learn how to spell them:

    cough   rough   through

    though   bough   thorough

Now write out each of the words, together with a word that rhymes with it. Begin:

    cough – off

4 Use a dictionary and find the correct spelling in each line:

    a. attention   attension   atention
    b. delicous   dilicious   delicious
    c. biginning   begining   beginning
    d. freind   friend   frenid
    e. frightened   fritened   frightend
    f. everywere   evrywhere   everywhere
    g. saucar   sorcer   saucer
    h. valuable   valuble   vallauble
    i. experence   experience   expereince
    j. whether   wether   whehter
    k. streme   streem   stream
    l. baught   bought   bougt

17 Apostrophes – shortened words

"What's the matter wi' Bill Jukes, you dog?" hissed Hook, towering over him.
"The matter wi' him is he's dead, stabbed," replied Cecco in a hollow voice.
(from *Peter Pan* by J. M. Barrie)

When you speak you often shorten two words and use them as one word. In writing, the **apostrophe** shows where letters have been missed out.
Which words have been shortened in the passage from Peter Pan?

Here are some more:
    I'm tired. (I *am* tired.)
    I'd like a snack. (I *would* like a snack.)
    I'll go now. (I *will* go now.)
    I'd had enough. (I *had* had enough.)
    You're next in the queue. (You *are* next in the queue.)
    I've forgotten what you said. (I *have* forgotten what you said.)

Learn and Remember

'It's' always means '*it is*'.
Not is shortened with some words.
    It's mine. (It *is* mine.)
    It isn't here. (It is *not* here.)
    She can't come. (She *cannot* come.)
    Don't leave me. (Do *not* leave me.)
    Weren't you in the cinema? (Were *not* you in the cinema?)
    Doesn't he boast? (Does *not* he boast?)
    You won't touch that, will you? ('Will not' becomes 'won't'.)

Starters

Write the following sentences using an apostrophe to shorten two words:

a. It is my fault.
b. You can not do that.
c. I did not see you.
d. Will you not come?
e. Do not cry.
f. I am not afraid.
g. I will not go.
h. There is no money here.
i. He had seen them before.
j. Would you not like some tea?

Written Practice

1 Write out these sentences in full without apostrophes:

a. He'll win.
b. Don't do that.
c. It's a fine day.
d. Here's my ticket.
e. Isn't it good?
f. They're coming now.
g. They weren't here.
h. We've done it.
i. There's no danger.
j. Won't that be enough?

2 Write out the following passage, putting in the apostrophes:
"Theyre coming now," whispered Julian. "Didnt you hear them just then?" "Youre right," answered Paul, "I hope itll all be over quickly. Theyve got all the advantages, havent they? Wouldnt it be great if they didnt see us? But I dont suppose theyd let us get away with it, do you?"

3 Write out this conversation between two friends. Use apostrophes to shorten words as they are spoken:
"I am going skating on Saturday," said James.
"You said you were not going, did you not?" said Ben.
James replied, "Well, I have changed my mind. Will you not come?"
"Oh! I do not know," said Ben. "I will come if I have enough money."

18 Apostrophes – Showing Possession

You use an **apostrophe** to show that something is owned by someone or something:

>The dog's paw was bleeding.
>A lady's handbag has been lost.
>The elephant's tusks were long and curved.
>My friend's house is over there.

See where the apostrophe goes when the item belongs to more than one person or animal:

>The dogs' tails wagged at the approach of their master.
>The girls' wages were paid today.
>The children's playground was empty.
>The women's overalls are on the pegs.

Guide

To decide whether the apostrophe comes before the 's' or after the 's', ask: Who owns it? Then put the apostrophe immediately after the owner. Look at this:

1 The boys book was stolen.
>*Ask:* Who owned the book?
>*Answer:* The boy.

Put the apostrophe after 'boy': The boy's book was stolen.

2 The girls heads nodded in agreement.
>*Ask:* Who owned the heads?
>*Answer:* The girls.

Put the apostrophe after 'girls': The girls' heads nodded in agreement.

Written Practice

1 Write out these sentences and put the apostrophe in the correct place:
- a. A policemans helmet rolled on the ground.
- b. I fastened the dogs collar round its neck.
- c. My fathers pipe was on the table.
- d. The childs foot slipped on the step.
- e. The womans hands were thin and cold.

2 Write out these sentences and put the apostrophe in the correct place:
- a. The eagles beak was sharp and curved.
- b. The speakers voice was loud and strong.
- c. The farmers dog followed behind him.
- d. The ladies prizes were presented to them by Lady Dunn.
- e. The cows tails swished about like fly swats.
- f. The clocks hands pointed to twelve.
- g. My sisters bedrooms are next to each other.
- h. A soldiers rifle lay on the ground.

3 Re-write these phrases using apostrophes.
Example: *the paws of my dog*   *my dog's paws*
- a. the ears of the horse
- b. the beaks of the parrots
- c. the coats of the women
- d. the tail of the tiger
- e. the tools of the workmen
- f. the books of the teacher
- g. the nose of the clown
- h. the boots of the soldiers
- i. the manes of the horses
- j. the boats of the fishermen

19 Comparing Adjectives

You often use **adjectives** to compare two people, things, creatures and places in many different ways:
> Simon is *taller* than John.
> Simon is *fatter* than John.
> John is *quicker* than Simon.
> John is *younger* than Simon.

> The first box is *bigger* than the second.
> The second box is *heavier* than the first.
> The second box is *stronger* than the first.

Sometimes you compare a person or thing with one other:
> Susan is *cleverer* than Richard.

Sometimes with many others:
> Robert is the *strongest* boy in the class.
> The cheetah is the *fastest* animal in the world.
> Ben Nevis is the *highest* mountain in the United Kingdom.

If the adjective is a short word, add -er and -est when comparing things:
> tall taller tallest   rich richer richest

If the adjective is a long word, use *more* or *most*:
> English is more interesting than history. Science is the most interesting of all.

Sometimes you use different words when comparing people or things:
> John is a *good* swimmer but a *bad* footballer.
> Susan is a *better* swimmer than John, but a *worse* footballer.
> Michael is the *best* swimmer but the *worst* footballer of all.

Other words which change when comparing things are:
> little less least   far farther farthest

Written practice

1 Write two sentences which compare the following pairs. The first one has been done for you:
    a. A fortnight and a week-end (length of time)
       A fortnight is longer than a week-end.
       A week-end is shorter than a fortnight.
    b. a metre and a centimetre (length)
    c. a cheetah and a horse (speed)
    d. a tea cup and a milk bottle (capacity)
    e. a bag of coal and a diamond (value)
    f. money and health (importance)
    g. rope and string (thickness)
    h. knife and razor (sharpness)

2 Write sentences giving the following information:
    a. the largest city in the United Kingdom
    b. the largest bird in the world
    c. the most common liquid in the world
    d. the smallest unit of length in common use (metric)
    e. the heaviest creature in the world

3 Write sentences containing these words:
    longest worst highest most important more frightened smallest

20 Collective Nouns

Collective nouns are used to name a group of many similar things. Here are some examples:

a *flock* of sheep   a *team* of footballers   a *bunch* of flowers
a *herd* of cattle   a *gang* of thieves   a *heap* of stones
a *litter* of pups   a *crowd* of spectators   a *string* of beads
a *swarm* of insects   a *band* of musicians

Starters

1 Which collective noun would you use instead of the word 'lot' in each of these phrases?

     a lot of people   a lot of elephants   a lot of birds
     a lot of ships   a lot of fishes   a lot of soldiers

2 Each of the following collective nouns can be used with more than one group.

     For example: a *flock* of sheep   a *flock* of birds.

With what are these collective nouns used:

     herd   pack   litter   team   set   swarm   school   gang

Written Practice

1 Write out these sentences, choosing the most suitable word from the brackets:

     a. The car slowed down behind a (party, herd, clump) of cattle.
     b. He paid for the (packet, bunch, bundle) of flowers and went out.
     c. To go abroad Mr Smith needed a new (swarm, pack, suit) of clothes.
     d. She was left an antique (chest, group, collection) of drawers by her grandmother.
     e. The cat had her (stack, litter, pile) of kittens in the woodshed.

2 To what do these refer? Look them up if necessary:

     bouquet   cluster   gaggle   flight   clutch   suite
     mob   pride   hand   covey   board   troop

21 Abstract Nouns

Abstract nouns are the names of ideas and qualities, things you cannot see or touch. Here are some abstract nouns:

I have an *idea*. What is the *question*? Here is a *plan*.
Give me an *answer*. It is a *fact*. I am in *love*.
the *fear* of darkness the *fury* of the storm the *fun* of the party

Starters

Think of six feelings that you sometimes have. Begin:
excitement . . . . .

Written Practice

1 Pick out the abstract nouns from each group of words:
   a. excitement   grass   magic   bread   belief   thought
   b. curiosity   sugar   flame   fact   opinion   agreement
   c. cowardice   bravery   earth   power   jealousy horse
   d. happiness   sorrow   joy   animal   anger   envy
   e. tank   hair   duty   fright   pity   generosity

2 Find out from a dictionary the meanings of *virtue* and *vice*, then write out two examples of each.

3 Write sentences using the words below:
   happiness   pity   sorrow   anger

4 Write the abstract nouns which are formed from these words:
   lazy   think   strong   jealous
   brave   stupid   weak   careless

Checkpoints

A

1. Punctuate each of these examples in two different ways, to give two different meanings:
    a. stop at the gate at the end of the garden you'll see a wheelbarrow
    b. Jill and I met you last week you had a cold
2. Read these clues. Use each answer in a sentence:
    a. an eleven-letter word which means *at once, straightaway*
    b. an adjective formed from *love*
    c. a word which means *starting*
3. Give three words which rhyme with:
    a. maul   ___ ___ ___
    b. fight ___ ___ ___
    c. high   ___ ___ ___
    d. know   ___ ___ ___
4. *Katie is taller than Marie who is taller than Pat.*
Draw a block graph showing who is tallest, and write a sentence about Pat.

    Mr Brown is poorer than Mr Black who is poorer than Mr Green.
Draw a bar graph showing who is richest. Write a sentence about Mr. Green.

B

1. Which group of animals are these collective nouns used for:
    pack   herd   troop   school   pride

2 What is the group name of each line of words. The first one is done for you:

China Italy England Australia Germany **countries**

   a. rose   daisy   violet   marigold   iris
   b. London   Paris   Moscow   Rome   Washington
   c. cabbage   beetroot   potato   cauliflower turnip
   d. Thames   Seine   Amazon   Niger   Danube
   e. gun   spear   rifle   sword   revolver
   f. taxi   bus   lorry   car   tractor
   g. flute   trumpet   trombone   violin   piano
   h. fir   holly   privet   pine   spruce

3 There is one abstract noun in each line. Which one is it?
   a. brick   build   idea   home
   b. mouth   discussion   tongue   head   face
   c. curious   curtain   curtail   curiosity curved

4 Put capitals, commas and full stops in these sentences:
   a. the fisherman caught a cod a crab and a mackerel
   b. the ingredients of the cake are flour sugar butter eggs currants and milk

5 Put apostrophes in the correct places:
   a. Grannys face was as white as a sheet.
   b. The childrens voices echoed in the tunnel.
   c. My horses coat was scratched and its ears torn.
   e. Dont touch Peters record; its not yours.

22 Speaking and Writing: Question Marks and Inverted Commas

Read this verse.
"Pussy cat, pussy cat, where have you been?"
"I've been to London, to see the Queen."
"Pussy cat, pussy cat, what did you there?"
"I frightened a little mouse under the chair."

Question marks (?) and **inverted commas** (" ") are used to put speaking into writing.

The Question Mark

Often a sentence is a question. The question mark shows the question in writing:

Where are you going?

Sometimes a question mark is the only way of telling a question. Read these two sentences aloud:

You're going tomorrow.
You're going tomorrow?

Inverted Commas

These show who is speaking. Look at this sentence:

John said Mary is angry.

Who is angry, John or Mary? It might be:

John said, "Mary is angry." or
"John," said Mary, "is angry."

Notice where the **commas** are.
Inverted commas go round the words that are actually spoken.
Commas go between the spoken words and the unspoken words.
Read the sentences:

    a. The leader said, "We'll carry on till dusk."

50

b. "We'll meet again," said Sue, "when I decide."
   c. "I'll be back in five minutes," he called.

Notice the punctuation and capital letters.
The spoken words begin with capital letters, but carry on with small letters (look at sentence b). Notice how commas show a pause between spoken and unspoken words.

Starters

Read these sentences to yourself. The punctuation will help you to read them:
   a. "Come here at once," she said.
   b. Will you please take these books back to the library?
   c. He said, very softly, "I've a secret to tell you."
   d. Where am I going? I'm going to town. Why do you ask?
   e. "I'm not going out," said Mother, "until it stops raining."

Written Practice

1 Write questions which begin with these words:
   which   do   will   what
   when   how   can   may
   are   why   where

   Give answers to your questions.

2 Write out these sentences, putting inverted commas, commas and question marks in the correct places:
   a. I will come he replied.
   b. Father said I've got a surprise for you.
   c. If you will help me he said you can keep the money.
   d. Where is my book he asked quietly.
   e. Are you going to the party she asked.
   f. Where is my pipe I've looked everywhere said Grandpa.

23 Spelling Guide

Here are some practical guides which will help you to spell many words. They are guides, not rules. The best way to use them is to:
    a. learn the guide and learn how to spell words that follow the guide
    b. learn the exceptions – the words that do not follow the guide

1 **Adding -ing:** if a word ends with -e, miss it out when adding -ing:

    come coming   joke   joking
    make making   promise promising
    give giving   starve starving
    save saving   cycle cycling

Exceptions
    singe singeing (otherwise it would be singing)
Where there is a vowel before the last -e:
    see seeing   canoe canoeing
    queue queueing

2 **Adding -ly:** do NOT leave out the final -e:

    love lovely   nice   nicely
    rare rarely   precise precisely
    late lately   definite definitely

3 **Adding -ing, -er or -ed:** when a word ends with a consonant, double the consonant:

    fit fitting   fitter   fitted
    dip dipping   dipper   dipped
    pot potting   potter   potted
    clap clapping   clapper   clapped
    slip slipping   slipper   slipped
    stir stirring   stirrer   stirred
    travel travelling   traveller travelled

Exceptions

Many words do not follow this guide:
- box   boxing   boxer   boxed
- play   playing   player   played
- row   rowing   rower   rowed

When there are TWO vowels before the last consonant, do NOT double the last letter:
- raid   raiding   raider   raided
- pour   pouring   pourer   poured
- shoot   shooting   shooter

Exception
- wool   woollen

Written Practice

1 Write ten words which end -e and miss it out when adding -ing.
   Example:
   wave – waving

2 Add -ing and -ed to each of these words:

step	plan	shop	knit	drip	delay
show	relax	display	strain	pit	riot
rain	shout	cycle	diet	save	drum

24 More spelling

This section is about *ie, ei* and *silent letters*.

'i' before 'e': when they are next to each other in a word, 'i' comes before 'e' except after 'c'.

    lie   die   pie   tie   diet
    field   flies   frieze   piece   niece
    shield   wield   shriek   belief   relief
    believe   relieve   achieve   friend

'e' comes before 'i' after 'c':

    receive   deceive   conceive   perceive
    receipt   deceit   conceit   ceiling

Exceptions

    either   neither   height
    eight   weight   freight
    seize   weird   eiderdown

Learn to Spell

1 Write out and learn the words in the i before e group.
2 Write out and learn the words in the e before i group.
3 Look at the exceptions. Notice the words:
    either and *neither*
    eight, weight and *freight*

Silent Letters

Silent letters are letters which you do not sound at all. Read these words, say them, and notice the silent letters:

silent letter	words
b	bomb comb doubt plumber
c	muscle scene yacht
g	sign reign gnaw gnat
gh	light eight high thought
h	honest hour heir John vehicle
k	know knee knot knife knit
l	talk calm palm would half
n	autumn column
p	pneumonia corps psalm
s	isle island aisle Basle
t	fasten listen ballet
w	wrong sword dawn answer

There are other words with silent letters as well as these. Watch out for them and remember them.

Written Practice

1 Write these numbers in words:
8   80   80th

2 Spell the words that fit these clues:
    a. to grab or grasp   s____
    b. to take possession of   r____
    c. accept the truth of   b____
    d. the top of a room   c____
    e. land surrounded by water   i____
    f. you use it to groom your hair   c____

25 Test Your Spelling

1 Write the following in words: 18, 44, 88th.
2 Write five words which end in –ough.
3 Add –ing to these words:
   bake   have   run   come   fold
   travel struggle capture paste   need
   increase grip   tumble   spin   begin
4 Write the words these signs represent in arithmetic:
   +   −   ×   ÷
5 Write five words which rhyme and end with the same patterns as these words.
   Example: raking, making, taking, baking, waking, faking
   hatch
   light
   witch
   hopping
   able
6 Spell the words that fit these clues:
   a. at once   i_____
   b. to burn slightly s_____
   c. adjective formed from 'wool'   w_____
   d. starting   b_____
   e. a cup and   s_____
7 Spell the plural of the following nouns:
   lion   woman   salmon   loaf   strawberry
   patch   spy   hero   piano   father-in-law
   plate   monkey filly   trousers dragonfly
   fox   potato princess story   landlady
   clock   half   sheep   storey   wretch
8 In these crosswords, the words cross at a silent letter. From the clues complete the crosswords. The first is done for you.

56

a. *across* bright and shining
   down frequently

                O
                F
G L I S T E N I N G
                E
                N

b. *across* a finger of your hand
   down you use this on your hair

c. *across* joint between ankle and hip
   down tied in string or rope

d. *across* a little old man from fairyland
   down you do this when you write your name

e. *across* perfume
   down you can cut paper with a pair

f. *across* incorrect
   down joint of the arm

g. *across* opposite of dark
   down twice nine

57

26 Idioms

James lost his head in the argument.

Which picture shows what is meant by the **idiom**, *lost his head*?

I tried to catch his eye as he entered the room.

What is the meaning of the idiom *to catch someone's eye*?

When you use an idiom, you use the words in a special way so that they have a different meaning from the meaning the words usually have.

58

Starters

What does each of these sentences mean?
   a. The thief was *caught red handed*.
   b. Let's *put our heads together* before we start work.
   c. Tell me what happened and stop *beating about the bush*.
   d. I made a mistake and I know Bob is *laughing up his sleeve*.
   e. I don't agree with the plan and I *wash my hands of it*.
   f. Pam was angry and refused to go to the party but she was only *cutting off her nose to spite her face*.
   g. Tim has some good points and he is *not as black as he is painted*.
   h. I can't *make head or tail* of what he is saying.
   i. Mum gets annoyed because my brother *won't do a hand's turn*.
   j. In the track events the Americans *swept the board*.

Written Practice

1 Here are some idioms and their meanings. Choose one and write a short passage to show you understand its meaning.
   a. crying for the moon
      wanting something that you can never get
   b. to have no leg to stand on
      to have no reason or excuse
   c. barking up the wrong tree
      be mistaken
   d. to have something hanging over your head
      to be threatened with something

2 Write sentences which show the meanings of the idioms below. The first has been done for you.
   It did not take James long to find his feet in his new school.
   turned over a new leaf.
   left no stone unturned.
   got cold feet.

27 Capital Letters

In different parts of this book there are references to **capital letters**. Here is a summary of when you use capitals:
1. the word I
2. at the beginning of a sentence.
3. proper nouns – the names of people, places, countries and special things such as ships, aeroplanes, horses
4. at the beginning of reported speech: He said, "Please take this."
5. for each important word in a title: *Treasure Island*
6. for days of the week, months of the year and festivals
7. at the beginning of lines of verse
8. for words indicating rank or profession when used with the person's name, e.g., Captain Miles led his company. Judge Lambert entered the court. (BUT: The captain was a good leader. The judge made notes.)

Starters

Which of these words should begin with capital letters?
alfred, banana, canada, dreadful, elephant, france, garage, hungary, igloo, jonathan, knowledge, labrador, moses, neptune, ostrich, peking, question, rudolph, sandy, treasure, viking, washington, xylophone, yacht, zambia.

Written Practice

1. Write out the following, using capitals and other punctuation marks in the correct places:
    a. tom ben and daniel are going to london on monday
    b. how did you enjoy your voyage to new york
    c. have you read watership down
    d. in the hall I saw the prime minister several judges professors and many other important people
    e. come with me said the guide and I will show you the most interesting place in venice

2. Copy and complete the form below, remembering to use capital letters correctly:

Your full name	
Address	
Date of birth	
Town and country of birth	
School	

Free for All

1 Write out the months of the year.

2 Write the names of the four countries of the British Isles.

3 Write the title of the most interesting book you have read.

4 What was the name of the best film you have ever seen?

5 Write out the passage below, putting in the capital letters:
mr john sebastian davis was seen with miss sonia eliza bentley walking down pond lane, off george street, chipping marsham, on wednesday 11th february at 10 p.m. they entered the cricketers' arms public house where they were later found by p.c. reginald manning.

28 Opposites

Using a different word

Sometimes a completely different word gives the opposite meaning:

I have *clean* hands.   Look at the dog's *dirty* paws.
This is *difficult* but that is *easy*.
This is a *cheap* coat but that one is *expensive*.
Mum *often* watches TV but she *seldom* goes to the pictures.

Adding a prefix

You can **add a prefix** to some words to give opposite meanings:

Anne is very *un*happy.   *Un*lock the door!
He came at an *in*convenient time.   Sally would not *dis*obey her father.
You are talking *non*sense.   It is *im*possible to do this puzzle.

Changing the prefix

You can **change the prefix** of some words to give the opposite meaning:

*In*side we are warm.   *Out*side it is cold and stormy.
The price of bread *in*creased, but the price of apples *de*creased.
I felt *dis*couraged but my family comforted and *en*couraged me.

Changing the suffix

You can change the **suffix** of some words to give the opposite meaning:
   Pam is a care*ful* worker but her brother is care*less*.
   A hammer is a use*ful* tool but this broken screwdriver is use*less*.

Written Practice

1 Give the opposites of:
   quick   sell   war   rise   absent
   go   ugly   first   tame   alive

2 Write two opposites for each of the following words. The first is done for you:
   kind   unkind   cruel   external ____ ____
   common   ____   ____   friend   ____ ____
   polite   ____   ____   correct   ____ ____
   sane   ____   ____   accurate ____ ____

3 Give the opposites of the words underlined:
   a. I went to the <u>entrance</u>.
   b. The stain was <u>visible</u> on the patterned carpet.
   c. There was <u>disorder</u> in the classroom.
   d. The plumber <u>connected</u> the water pipes.
   e. My mother would <u>approve</u> of the way I am working.

4 We often use a pair of opposites in ordinary speech. Write sentences using these opposites:
   come and go   life and death   off and on
   dead or alive   stop and start   give and take
   up and down   buy and sell   in and out

Checkpoints

A

1 Punctuate the following conversation using inverted commas, commas and question marks:

    Are there no prisons asked Scrooge.
    Plenty of prisons said the gentleman laying down the pen again.
    And the union workhouses demanded Scrooge. Are they still in operation
    They are. Still returned the gentleman I wish I could say they were not.

2 Write the plurals of:
    a. fly baby daisy diary dairy
    b. church lass arch fox ash
    c. shelf half leaf loaf yourself
    d. key donkey day toy chimney
    e. potato echo hero tomato volcano

3 By adding a prefix, give the opposites of:
    a. happy reliable popular conscious
    b. correct visible justice distinct
    c. like appear connect advantage
    d. possible probable perfect patient

4 Add –ing to:
    play begin tap fill find sit
    make see mine tire fade take

B

1 Change the suffix to give the opposite of:
   helpless thoughtful useful careless harmful

2 Rewrite these sentences by adding a prefix to one word, so that they mean the opposite:
   a. I am very happy.
   b. Pam is a contented person.
   c. These goods are perfect.
   d. The old man often talks sense.

3 Write the answers to these clues, and underline the silent letter in each word:
   a. Used to do hair.
   b. The day after Tuesday.
   c. The flat of your hand.
   d. The season before winter.
   e. Often used with a fork.

4 Add –er to these words:
   begin talk run travel throw sing

5 Give the opposites of the words underlined:
   a. Boating is prohibited on this lake.
   b. If the temperature changes the metal will expand.
   c. The alteration in our plans is a temporary change.
   d. She is a modest person.

6 Pick out two pairs of opposites in each line:
   a. deny accuse admit inside sideways outside
   b. inferior cap forbid superior hat allow
   c. sudden freedom slope gradual captivity up

29 Similar Words

You use many words that have similar meanings. Here are some pictures of words that are roughly the same in meaning. Make up a sentence about each picture:

jump   leap   vault

spring

bound

Many groups of words mean nearly the same, but not quite:
    I *saw* a chicken crossing the road.
    Terry *looked* at his dad's photographs.
    We all *watched* T.V.
    John *stared* with open mouth as the ladder fell.
    Did you *notice* any difference between the two pictures?
    For several minutes I *gazed* at the beautiful countryside below me.
    She *observed* a man climbing through the window.
    We *perceived* that we were not welcome.

Starters

1 Rewrite these sentences using simpler words for the words underlined. Keep the same meaning.
   a. The car travelled at a great velocity.
   b. He tried to compel me to go.
   c. He is a courageous man.
   d. The climber was overcome with fatigue.

2 Write shorter words which mean the same as:
   vacant celebrated avaricious demonstrate necessity

Written Practice

1 Use the words *hear* (hearing) and *listen* (listening) to complete these sentences:
   a. I am ____ but I cannot ____ a sound.
   b. I can ____ pop music in the background but I'm not ____ to it.
Use *see* (saw) and *look* (looked, looking) to complete these sentences:
   c. I ____ everywhere but I didn't ____ it.
   d. I ____ the purse but I was not ____ for it.
Use *touch* (touched) and *feel* (felt) to complete these sentences:
   e. He ____ my pocket but I never ____ anything.
   f. I ____ a sharp pain when I ____ the wire.

2 Pick out the odd word in each set:
   a. tired weary exhausted crying fatigued
   b. break trip snap fracture shatter
   c. tall high lofty elevated vast
   d. copy imitate mimic sing impersonate
   e. break shake tremble shiver vibrate
   f. dive plunge swoop climb plummet
   g. throw cast drop sling hurl
   h. start begin commence embark finish

30 Building Words, Prefixes and Suffixes

Slowly Larry opened his eyes. He became *dimly* aware of his *surroundings*. He was in a small, *unlit* room with damp and *discoloured* walls and there was a smell of *mustiness* and decay. He seemed to be lying on an *uncomfortable* and *unusually lumpy* old mattress. He tried to stand up but his head spun with *giddiness* and his eyes and temples throbbed *painfully*.

As you can see from the passage, you build many words by adding **prefixes** and suffixes. In section 28 you learned how prefixes and suffixes are used to make opposites. Here you can learn how they are used in word-building.

Read the stages of word building below:

Word	Add a prefix	Add a suffix	Add a prefix and a suffix
kind	unkind	kindness	unkindness
		kindly	unkindly
happy	unhappy	happiness	unhappiness
		happily	unhappily
perfect	imperfect	perfectly	imperfectly
		perfection	imperfection
honest	dishonest	honestly	dishonestly
		honesty	dishonesty
normal	abnormal	normality	abnormality

There are many other prefixes and suffixes. Here are some of them:

Prefixes: pro- (protect) con- (contain) pre- (prefix)
fore- (forecast) sub- (submarine)

Suffixes: -ed (stopped) -ing (happening) -er (runner)
-ment (enjoyment) -y (lumpy)

Starters

Make six columns and write in each at least five examples of:

Word beginning *Word ending*
dis- un- im- -ness -ment -ly

Written Practice

1 Write ten words that end with the suffix -ward(s). Begin: upward

2 Write out the following passage, putting the right endings on the words in brackets:
(Quiet) and (smooth) the boat (glide) through the water. David was (pull) on the oars as hard as he could, but kept (think) he could go even (fast). Time was (run) out. He was tense with (excite) and (nervous) and he knew that as soon as he (stop) (row) he would feel (extreme) tired and would (probable) be unable to go on.

3 Use prefixes and suffixes to build other words from:
possible   direct   agree   appear   pure
sane   eat   legal   hope   content

4 Re-write these words and underline the prefixes. Look up the meanings of the words:
underground   propose   preposition   foretell
bicycle   translate   subterranean   mistake

5 Re-write these words, underline the suffixes, and look up the meanings of the words:
countess   cigarette   fighter   servant
careless   eatable   duckling   magnify

31 Comparative Adverbs

You often use adverbs to compare how actions are performed:
>Sam eats *more* than Tim.
>James answered *more intelligently* than Bob.
>He slept *more soundly* than I did.
>Betty searched *most carefully* of all.
>Ruth dances *more gracefully* than Sue.
>I climbed *higher* than Brian.
>He ran *faster* than I did.
>This sack of coal weighs *heavier* than that one.
>Pat tried *harder* than her friend.
>Ann tried *hardest* of all.
>I did *better* than before.

When adverbs end in -ly you use *more* and *most* to make comparisons. But you add -er and -est to some adverbs.
>climbs *higher* (highest)   ran *faster* (fastest)

Notice these:

He did *well*.	She did *better*.	Dan did *best* of all.
He gave *little*.	She gave *less*.	Dan gave *least* of all.
I like him very *much*.	I like Tom *more*.	I like Bob *most* of all.

Starters

Fill in the comparatives of the adverbs underlined in these sentences:
a. Rufus ate <u>greedily</u>. He ate ____ than the others. He ate ____ of all of them.
b. John did his work <u>well</u>. He did his work ____ than before. He did his work ____ of all.
c. Janice writes <u>badly</u>. She writes ____ than her friend. She writes ____ of all in the class.
d. This car travels <u>fast</u>? Which of the two cars goes ____? Which car goes ____ of all?

Written Practice

1 Here is a block graph showing the points scored by Dave, Tom and Jack in an athletics competition:

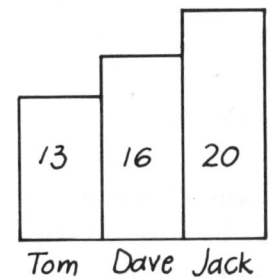

```
         ┌────┐
    ┌────┤    │
┌───┤    │    │
│13 │ 16 │ 20 │
└───┴────┴────┘
 Tom  Dave Jack
```

Write six sentences comparing the points that they scored. Begin: Dave scored more than Tom.

2 Fill in the spaces with a suitable adverb:
   a. This apple tastes ____ than that one.
   b. The blue car starts ____ than that one.
   c. Out of the whole class it was Mary who ran ____.
   d. Take this pencil, it writes ____ than that one.
   e. Which is the ____, chocolate, sugar or honey?
   f. A dog eats ____ than a bird.
   g. Jack Blunt snored ____ than his wife.
   h. Billy cried, Jean cried but little Josh cried ____ of all.
   i. There were ten competitors and Mark jumped ____.

3 Write sentences using the following:
   a. more quietly   e. more kindly
   b. most carefully   f. hardest
   c. more sweetly   g. fastest
   d. most fiercely   h. more noisily

32 Similes

How large unto a tiny fly
Must little things appear!
A rosebud like a feather bed,
Its prickle like a spear.
(from 'The Fly' by Walter de la Mare)

Similes are comparisons which use the words 'like' and 'as'. They compare two people or things which are alike in one special way:

>She was trembling *like a leaf*. Her face was *as pale as death*.
>The kite rose *like a bird*. Jo has been *as good as gold*.
>He drove *like a maniac*. That story is *as old as the hills*.
>Dick ate *like a pig*. The stallion was *as black as the night*.

Using Similes

You can make your writing more lively if you can think of similes of your own to use.
If a bucket leaked badly, you could say:
>*It's useless. This bucket leaks. It won't hold water.*

or you could use similes and say:
>*This bucket leaks like a sieve. It's as full of holes as a colander.*

Starters

1 Complete these similes by using one of the following words:
wise fresh hard fierce clear light fit bold
   a. as ____ as a lion   e. as ____ as an owl
   b. as ____ as brass   f. as ____ as nails
   c. as ____ as a daisy   g. as ____ as crystal
   d. as ____ as a fiddle   h. as ____ as a feather

2 Make up endings for these similes:
- a. as green as ____
- b. as dull as ____
- c. as mad as ____
- d. as silly as ____
- e. as easy as ____
- f. as nervous as ____
- g. as smooth as ____
- h. as hard as ____
- i. as pretty as ____
- j. as hot as ____

Written Practice

1 Complete these sentences with the following words:
snow lead clockwork ice ox toast rock mouse
- a. My hands are as cold as ____.
- b. The basket was heavy as ____.
- c. The lighthouse flashed as regular as ____.
- d. I sat by the fire and my feet were as warm as ____.
- e. Mary had a little lamb, its fleece was white as ____.
- f. Jenny sat behind the curtain, as quiet as a ____.
- g. The man was huge and as strong as an ____.
- h. The icing on that cake is as hard as ____.

2 Use these similes in sentences:
- a. like a bull in a china shop
- b. as calm as a mill pond
- c. like a jelly
- d. as slow as a snail

3 Complete these sentences:
- a. He burst into the room like ____.
- b. My bike tyre was a flat as ____.
- c. The blade of the dagger was as sharp as ____.
- d. Snow covered the ground like ____.
- e. Billy blushed as red as ____.

4 Read the poem again. Imagine a tiny fly in your living room. Write some short sentences or a poem about how you think things in your home would appear to the fly.

33 Time Conjunctions

Section 10 in this book is about joining words or **conjunctions**.
You can use **conjunctions of time** to join two sentences or parts of a sentence in different ways.

> He had eaten his lunch. He fell asleep.
> He fell asleep *after* he had eaten his lunch.
> *After* he had eaten his lunch he fell asleep.

Here are some more time conjunctions:

> when before since until whenever as while

Pick out the time conjunctions in these sentences:

> I switched off the light before I got into bed.
> They have been good friends since they first met at school.
> My aunt gives me sweets whenever I go to see her.
> The driver was getting into his taxi when he slipped.
> As I was writing my friend nudged me.
> While the building burned, faces appeared at the window.
> You must stay here until I tell you to go.

Starters

Re-write the first three sentences above, putting the time conjunctions in different positions but keeping the meaning the same.

Written Practice

1. Use suitable time conjunctions and join these pairs of sentences:
   a. I wash my hands. I eat my meal.
   b. Judith swept t e carpet. Father washed up.
   c. I feel very weak. I have been ill.
   d. Tom will not come here again. You apologize.
   e. The door bell rang. We were sitting down to dinner.

2. Re-write each sentence putting the time conjunction in a different position but without changing the meaning of the sentence:
   a. My friend stumbled as she stepped out of the house.

b. We all have a good time whenever my uncle comes to our house.
   c. Until we meet again we won't tell anyone of our plan.
   d. I will think it over before I decide.
   e. I shall go to the doctor again when I have finished the medicine.

3 Use a suitable time conjunction to finish each of these sentences:
   a. I was standing by the door ____ a bull came round the corner.
   b. We shall wait here ____ we are told to go.
   c. Jane has suffered from headaches ____ she was a child.
   d. ___ I was speaking, Tom interrupted me.
   e. ____ we are waiting, we can listen to the news.

4 Match the two parts of the following sentences:

While we sat there waiting,	we shall have to manage as we are.
After the party was over,	before we go to sleep.
Whenever he passed,	since his father died.
Until something turns up,	we did not know what was happening outside.
We get ino bed	we went home by taxi.
I was walking down the road	he would give a friendly smile.
I met him in the street	when a thought suddenly struck me.
I have only got to know him	as I was coming home.

5 Complete the following sentences:
   a. I was waiting for my friend while ____.
   b. After my mother gave me my spending money ____.
   c. I opened the door as ____.
   d. Before he could do anything ____.
   e. Since they went away ____.

75

34 Metaphors

The wind was a torrent of darkness among the gusty trees,
The moon was a ghostly galleon tossed upon cloudy seas,
The road was a ribbon of moonlight over the purple moor,
And the highwayman came riding up to the old inn door.
(from 'The Highwayman' by Sir Henry Newbolt)

The poem uses four **metaphors**. It compares:
>the moon to a ghostly galleon
>the clouds to a rough sea
>the wind to a dark torrent
>the road to a ribbon stretched across the moor

If he had used a simile the poet would have written:
>The moon was *like* a ghostly galleon

But he used a metaphor and wrote that the moon *was* a ghostly galleon.

>**Simile** She is as busy as a bee.
>**Metaphor** She is a busy bee.
>**Simile** He is as stupid as a donkey.
>**Metaphor** He is a stupid donkey.
>**Simile** He is like a live wire.
>**Metaphor** He is a live wire.

Here are some more metaphors:
>*My blood froze* when I saw the crash.
>When Jill's pet died, it *broke her heart*.
>I waited in the dark *with my heart in my mouth*.

Written Practice

1 In each set write out the two sentences that mean the same:
   a. He was delighted and excited.
      He was mad.
      He was over the moon.
   b. She was living in a slum.
      She was down in the dumps.
      She was depressed.
   c. Tom is very hard-hearted.
      Tom is tough and brave.
      Tom has no feelings.
   d. She came home walking on air.
      She came home light-headed.
      She came home very happy.
   e. Dan turned a deaf ear to me.
      Dan was rather deaf and could not hear me.
      Dan would not listen to me.

2 Write another sentence which means the same as:
   a. He is a wet blanket.
   b. She is full of beans.
   c. My blood boiled when I saw what he was doing.
   d. He is a big fish in a small pond.
   e. At football Smith was a giant.

Checkpoints

A

1 Give three-letter words which have the same or nearly the same meaning as:
   a. purchase weep attempt cunning carve
   b. enemy gigantic also melancholy curve

2 Add a prefix and a suffix to each of these words, and write sentences using each new word:
Example: self unselfish My sister is unselfish.
   a. agree b. appear c. certain

3 Complete the following similes:
   a. as ____ as a lion
   b. as cunning as a ____
   c. as blind as a ____
   d. as ____ as a mule
   e. as slippery as an ____

4 Use one of these conjunctions to complete the sentences:
   as while before after when
   a. You must find some cotton ____ I can sew this button on.
   b. Will you wash up ____ I sew the button on your coat?
   c. We'll go shopping ____ I have finished my work.
   d. Tom came in ____ I was going out.
   e. Come and sit down ____ you have taken your coat off.

5 Give the comparisons of these adverbs:
   well much loudly happily

B

1 Change the word underlined for a simpler word that means the same:
   a. I asked my father for <u>assistance</u> with my work.
   b. He stumbled at the <u>commencement</u> of the race.
   c. I <u>comprehend</u> what you are saying.
   d. We have an <u>abundant</u> supply of food.

2 In a competition Tim scored 8 points, Bobby 12 points and Sam 6 points.
   Complete the sentences:
   a. Sam scored ____ than Bobby.
   b. Bobby scored ____ than Tim.
   c. Sam scored ____ of all.
   d. Sam did ____ than Tim.
   e. Bobby did ____ of all.

3 Complete these similes:
   a. ____ as rock
   b. ____ as a bell
   c. ____ as a razor
   d. ____ as a mouse
   e. ____ as a horse

4 Use the conjunctions *since* or *until* to complete the sentences:
   a. We'll stay here ____ Mother arrives.
   b. It's been a long time ____ I saw you.
   c. ____ we don't know the answer, we'd better ask someone.
   d. We've been friends ____ the first time we met.
   e. Do not leave the house ____ I return.

35 Homonyms

Never pitch a tent on a cricket pitch.

What do the two words 'pitch' mean in this sentence?
Homonyms are words which are spelt the same but have different meanings.

Look at these pictures:

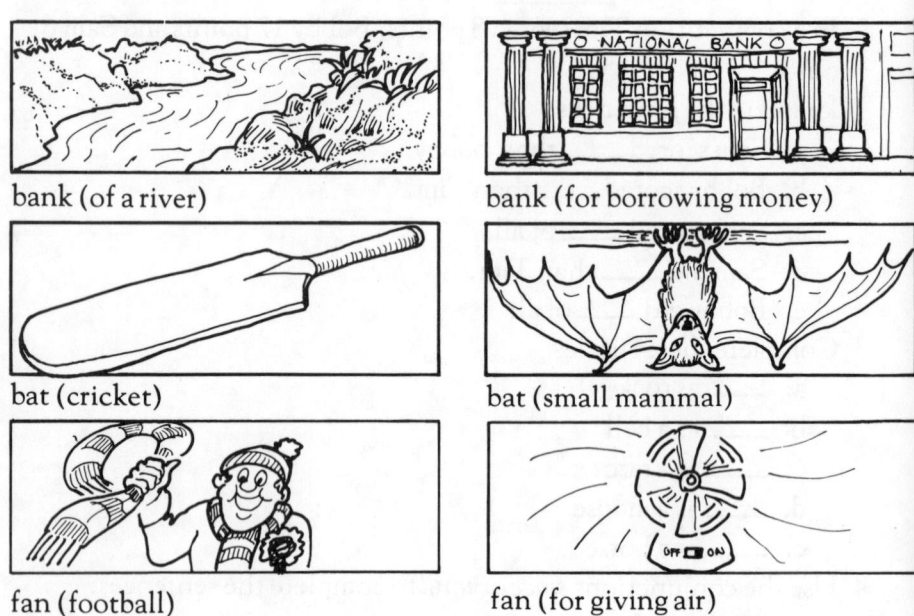

bank (of a river)

bank (for borrowing money)

bat (cricket)

bat (small mammal)

fan (football)

fan (for giving air)

Tom has broken both *arms*.
The soldiers carried their *arms* into battle.
Grey squirrels strip the *bark* from trees.
The watchdog gave a warning *bark*.
The motorist paid his £10 *fine*.
Barry has a *fine* guitar.
Tomorrow the weather will be *fine*.

Starters

Draw pictures to show you know two different meanings of the words:
jam wave page hatch

Written Practice

Homonyms can be nouns, adjectives or verbs:
>The joiner cut the wood with his *saw*. I *saw* him doing it.
>She is a *kind* person. She is the *kind* I like.

1 a. Write sentences and use these words as *nouns*:
>lie   watch   sink   grave   plain

b. Write sentences and use these words as *verbs*:
>lie   watch   sink   catch   long

c. Write sentences and use these words as *adjectives*:
>grave   long   plain

2 Read the sentences:
>a. The machine *ground* the rock to powder.
>b. I carried the empty basket. It was *light*.
>c. Ann started to *swing* on the gate.
>d. Bob is going on a *trip* to the seaside.

Now write sentences using *ground* as a noun, *light* as a noun, *swing* as a noun, *trip* as a verb.

Free for All

You will find many examples of homonyms in a dictionary. Usually the homonyms have a small figure to show different meanings, like this:
>$lock_1$ tuft of hair
>$lock_2$ fastening for door or drawer
>$lock_3$ part of a canal shut off by gates

Look in a dictionary and find the different meanings of these homonyms:

$clip_1$ fastener $jumper_1$
$clip_2$ $jumper_2$

$cape_1$ headland $record_1$
$cape_2$ $record_2$
                           $record_3$

$club_1$ organisation
$club_2$

$fair_1$
$fair_2$

36 Meaning and Emphasis

Read this poem aloud:
Swarthy smoke-blackened smiths, smudged with soot,
Drive me to death with the din of their banging.
Men never knew such a noise at night!
Such clattering and clanging, such clamour of scoundrels!
Crabbed and crooked, they cry, "Coal! Coal!"
And blow with their bellows till their brains burst.
(from 'The Smiths' by Brian Stone)

See how the sound of the words in the poem help build up the picture.
You can give **emphasis** to what you say and write in several ways:
1 by repeating the same letter-sound in several words close together
 (this is called **alliteration**)
   *S*warthy *s*moke-blackened *s*miths, *s*mudged with *s*oot,
   *D*rive me to *d*eath with the *d*in of their banging.
2 by repeating the same word:
   Such clattering and clanging, *such* clamour of scoundrels!
   Crabbed and crooked, they cry, "*Coal! Coal!*"
3 by repeating the meaning in different words:
   clattering and clanging   *crabbed and crooked*
   rant and rave   *fast and furious*
4 by using opposites together:
   it comes and goes   *through thick and thin*
   a matter of life and death *the long and short of it*

Starters

1 What are the opposites that you would use with these words:
   more or ___   here and ___
   to and ___   off and ___
   dead or ___   stop and ___

2 Pick out the examples of alliteration in the poem.

Written Practice

1 Here are some words whose sounds suggest their meanings:

    splash   crash   grunt   swish   cuckoo
    zoom   plop   screech bang   squelch
    ping   chug   clank   puff   crunch

Look them up in a dictionary. Use each one in a sentence.

2 Write sentences using these pairs of words:
- a. puff and blow
- b. hue and cry
- c. slip and slide
- d. ways and means

3 Write sentences using each of these phrases:
- a. on and on
- b. slower and slower
- c. round and round
- d. over and over
- e. through and through
- f. more and more

4 What words would you use to describe the sound of:
- a. a bell
- b. a plate falling on the floor
- c. a waterfall
- d. a foghorn
- e. rain falling

Write sentences using the words you have chosen.

37 Making New Verbs

You make new verbs by adding a word or two to a common verb. You use many of these new verbs every day.
Suppose a piece of paper caught fire and you stopped it burning. You would say, "I put the fire out." A word for 'put out' is *extinguish*, but very few people would say, "I extinguished the fire."

New verbs from *put*
    put on (clothes)   put on (speed)
    put off (doing something) put back (the clock)

New verbs from *give*
    give in (to someone)   give away (a secret)
    give up (trying)   give off (a smell)

New verbs from *get*
    get up (in the morning)   get away (from a place)
    get on (a bicycle)   get out (from your pocket)
    get along with (a person) get off (a bus)
    get out (of a house)   get on (with your work)
    get on (in life)   get over (a difficulty)

There are many more like these.

Starters

What do these expressions mean? What other words might you use for the words in italics?

    a. *put forward* an idea   f. *put out* to sea
    b. *let off* steam   g. *get into* trouble
    c. *get out* of doing something h. *get off* with a warning
    d. *get at* somebody   i. *get over* an illness
    e. *go in for* a race   j. *put in for* a rise

Written Practice

1 Complete these sentences by adding a word(s) to each verb:
   a. His hands were round my throat, but I would not give ____.
   b. People were always telling me to get ____ my work, but I kept putting it ____.
   c. The old man was heartbroken by his wife's death and took a long time to get ____ it.
   d. My mother did not want to let us go, but we got ____ her in the end.
   e. We could not get any more food, and soon we would run ____ altogether.
   f. There were no plays in the library, so we made one ____.

2 Write sentences showing that you understand what the following verbs mean:
   fall out (with a friend)   make up (a story)
   catch up (with a criminal)   run out (of ideas)
   let down (a friend)   get into (a temper)

38 Abbreviations

Abbreviations are shortened words. You see them on signs, posters, in newspapers and in letters.

Pick out the abbreviations in the drawings below. What does each one mean?

CHERRY AVE   AA   MILL RD

LEE ST   BBC1 BBC2 ITV   RR

AD 1867   DR A HARRIS

An abbreviation often has a full stop after it.
What do these abbreviations stand for?

    P.C. Wood arrested the thief.
    John added a P.S. to the letter to his friend.
    At the bottom of the first page he wrote P.T.O.
    Who is the President of the U.S.A.?

Starters

Write the abbreviations of:
    road street avenue place crescent square

Written Practice

1 What are the full names of these organisations:
    B.R.   N.C.B.   R.A.F.   C.I.D.   R.N.
    T.U.C.   A.A.A.   F.A.   E.E.C.   B.P.
2 On a map find these places and write out their names in full:
    U.K.   U.S.A.   U.S.S.R.   G.B.   I.O.M.   I.O.W.

39 Contractions

Some words are often shortened. The original long word is hardly used at all. You say:
>bus instead of *omnibus*
>mac instead of *macintosh*
>pram instead of *perambulator*

and there are many others like these.

Starters

Write the full words of the contractions underlined:
  a. Here is a <u>photo</u> of my mother.
  b. The Wright brothers flew the first <u>plane</u>.
  c. I had a <u>phone</u> call from my friend.

Written Practice

1 What are the contractions of these words? Use each one in a sentence:
>veterinary surgeon   popular music
>gymnasium   promenade

2 Rewrite these sentences using a contraction where suitable:
  a. On Saturday I am going for a ride on my bicycle.
     If it rains I shall take my mackintosh.
     When I come home I shall watch the television.
  b. I like popular music.
     I do not think I could sing into a microphone.
  c. There is a public house at the corner of our street.
  d. In the park there was a demonstration of motor car workers.

40 Word Building

Compound Words

The simplest way of word building is to put two words together and make a new word. New words made in this way are called **compound words**:

fire   man   a fireman

Look at these words and notice how two words are joined together to make a new word:

schoolgirl motorway lipstick lighthouse matchbox crossword

Sometimes the two words are joined with a hyphen and sometimes two separate words are used as a noun.

1 Two words joined together:

    She wore a *sheepskin* coat.   My mother made a *pancake*.

    We went to London on the *motorway*.   I like to do a *crossword*.

2 Two words joined with a hyphen:

    Mother works *part-time* in a laundry.   He's a *know-all*.

    He wanted to *hitch-hike* round Europe.   Nylon is a *man-made* fibre.

3 Two separate words used as a noun:

    My dad went to a *boxing match*.   The *waiting room* was empty.

    I went to the *booking office* at the station.

Combining words

Some words can be combined with several other words. Each new word has a special meaning. For example, using the word *shaped*:

    heart-shaped star-shaped pear-shaped kidney-shaped

    leaf-shaped

Other combining words: -power -wise fore- -mate

    The wheel turned *clockwise*.   He poked me with his *forefinger*.

    What *horsepower* is your car?   My father's *workmate* is ill.

Starters

1 Use these words in pairs and make at least five compound words:
   table shop ache foot keeper
   cloth light ball tooth flash
2 Pick out the compound words in these sentences:
   a. The detective spotted a fingerprint on the window.
   b. There was a rather uninspiring display of knitwear on the counter.
   c. Mum used a tape-measure from her sewing box.
   d. The long-range weather forecast was gloomy as usual.
   e. We got a snack from the takeaway.

Written Practice

1 Write sentences for each of the compound words below, like this:
matchbox

   a. Dad struck a *match* and lit the bonfire.
   b. All my old records are in a *box* in the attic.
   c. At first the beetle Alphonso was kept in a *matchbox*.

Now do the same with these words:
   lighthouse earthquake manhole lookout thunderstorm

2 Use each of these compound words in a sentence:
   record player ground floor knee-deep crash barrier
   rubbish heap weekend cricket bat kind-hearted

Free for All

Find as many examples of the following combining words as possible:
   -time -proof -free -handed
   -sized -wise cross- fore-

Set them out like this:
   -mate: shipmate, playmate, schoolmate, workmate
   -power: manpower, horsepower, atomic power,
            nuclear power, world power

41 Nouns as Adjectives

Dirty British coaster with a salt-caked smoke stack
Butting through the Channel in the mad March days,
With a cargo of Tyne coal,
Road-rail, pig-lead,
Firewood, iron-ware, and cheap tin trays.
(from 'Cargoes' by John Masefield)

Many nouns are used as adjectives. How many can you see in the poem above?
Football is a noun. But you talk about:
    a *football* match, a *football* jersey, a *football* team, *football* boots,
    a *football* player, a *football* pitch, a *football* referee.
Tea is grown in India and Sri Lanka. But you talk about:
    a *tea* cup, a *tea* bag, a *tea* party,
    a *tea* spoon, a *tea* towel, *tea* time.

Starters
Here are some nouns which you can use as adjectives. Write at least two examples of each one:
    paper   farm   table   house   Christmas
    glass   dog   school   milk   television

Written Practice
Write out the sentences below, underlining the nouns used as adjectives. There are at least two in each sentence:
  a. Mr Bloggs left his car in the car park, picked up his cigarette case and tobacco pouch, and went to buy a ticket for the boat train.
  b. After her morning coffee Mother tidied the kitchen, cleared the plate rack, made a bread pudding and got out the cake stand.
  c. Eventually John found the bus timetable on the coffee table.
  d. Mr Brown mended the light switch, the coat stand and the carpet sweeper.
  e. The curtain rings were in a flower pot beside a pile of picture frames, rag dolls, china plates and old newspaper articles.

42 Slang

Clear off! You're crackers!

All right! Keep your hair on!

These people are talking in **slang**. Everyone talks in slang sometimes. At work people talk of *clocking on* and *knocking off*. Prisoners talk about the *nick* and a *grass*. Find out what these expressions mean.

There are many other common words and phrases which are used in everyday talking and writing:

    good for nothing   stuck up   in bad shape
    out of sorts   keen on   a bird

What do they mean?

Written Practice

1 Write phrases which mean the same as:
    kick the bucket   a drop out   skip it
    a walk out   on the box   cough it up

2 Write sentences which mean the same as:
    a. I'm fed up!
    b. Where's my grub?
    c. He told me to pack it in, so I shut up.
    d. I tell you, it put the wind up me.
    e. I'm not going to carry the can for this.
    f. I saw a good movie at the flicks last night.

43 Overworked Words

[Illustration: People saying "Its a nice day", "She's a nice girl", "They live in a nice house", "He's wearing a nice sweater", "Those are nice flowers"]

In the pictures above everyone is using the word *nice*. Can you think of a more interesting word that could be used in each case? Sometimes these words are used when others may be better:

That cake is *nice*, Mother.
That cake is delicious, Mother.
We had a *really nice* evening.
We had a most enjoyable evening.
That was a *good* lecture, Professor Blythe.
That was an interesting lecture, Professor Blythe.
She has *a lot of* friends.
She has many friends.

Written Practice

1 Write out these sentences finding two different words to replace the one underlined. The first is done for you:
    a. This is a good plan.
       This is a clever, well thought-out plan.
    b. We had a nice holiday.
    c. I'm reading a good book.
    d. Picasso was a great painter.
    e. They have a lovely garden.
    f. He is a bad man.
    g. The boxer was a big man.
    h. We all had a lot to eat.

2 Write out the following, changing each word underlined:
    a. I've got a funny feeling that I've been here before.
    b. Inside the big box there were lots of beads.
    c. What a funny thing to say!
    d. Will you grow up to be a great musician?
    e. He has a good job.
    f. I thought she was a really nice girl.

3 *really   awfully   terribly*
Some people use these words instead of 'very'.
Look up the meaning of each word in a dictionary and then read these sentences:
    He is a really good actor.
    The food tasted really sweet.

    She is awfully kind.
    Our parents were awfully worried when we were late.

    This is terribly poor work.
    "You are terribly kind," she said.
Can you think of better words to use instead?

44 Homophones

"I'll be in the Isle of Man by tonight," thought the bride as she walked up the aisle.

Homophones are words that have the same sound but different meanings and spellings. There are many words like this. Pick out t e homophones in the sentence at the top of the page.

flower   flour   hair   hare

key   quay   leak   leek

We are not *allowed* to read *aloud*.
The boy *blew* a whistle and waved a *blue* flag.
She went *by* herself to *buy* some sweets.
I *knew* you would like my *new* coat.
A *mist* came down at dusk. We *missed* the bus.
Where are *their* books? I saw them over *there*.
Two friends went *to* the concert. I went *too*.

94

The roses had a lovely *scent*. My friend *sent* me a letter.
A *cent* is a coin in the U.S.A.

Starters

Sort these words into pairs of homophones:

    board   cellar   knot   grown   course
    made   hall   herd   fowl   haul
    heard   buoy   coarse   maid   seller
    not   foul   groan   boy   bored

Written Practice

1 Write sentences showing you know the meanings of these words:
    a. rode road rowed
    b. rain reign rein
    c. through threw
    d. tail tale
    e. feet feat

2 Complete these sentences with the correct word:
    a. The old man was very ____ (weak, week).
    b. There is a ____ (sale, sail) at the Co-op.
    c. We decided to ____ (higher, hire) a car for our holiday.
    d. I am going to ____ (meet, meat) her at the station.
    e. Bread is made with ____ (flower, flour).
    f. He ____ (nose, knows) I am telling the truth.
    g. I knew you ____ (would, wood) come.
    h. I can ____ (hear, here) you from ____ (hear, here).
    i. Mother decided to ____ (die, dye) the curtains.
    j. The knife was ____ (maid, made) of fine ____ (steal, steel).

Free for All

Here are more difficult homophones. Find out what each word means
   and use it in a sentence:

    practice practise   stationary stationery   faint feint
    current currant   lightening lightning   kernel colonel

Checkpoints

A

1 Write two sentences giving two meanings for each of:
   light fine jan kind watch

2 Use another verb instead of the words underlined:
   a. The prisoner got away through a small hole in the wire.
   b. I am not going to fall out with you.
   c. I won't go against you, either.

3 What are the abbreviations for:
   a. the days of the week
   b. the last four months of the year
   c. before noon and afternoon

4 Re-write these sentences, using better words instead of the words underlined:
   a. It's a nice dress.
   b. You are nice.
   c. What a nice thing to say!
   d. She's a good actress but a bad cook.

5 Re-write each pair of sentences using homophones instead of the words underlined:
   a. The train was stopped.
      I need some writing materials.
   b. The letters and parcels went by air.
      The job was advertised for a man or woman.
   c. We took the shortest way to York.
      A mouse nibbled the underground part of the plant.
   d. He stood in the rain with his head uncovered.
      A grizzly is a large fierce animal in North America.

B

1 Make a new verb beginning *put* or *give* instead of the verb underlined:
   a. On the straight road the police car <u>increased</u> speed.
   b. Will you <u>distribute</u> these leaflets?
   c. He was losing the fight but would not <u>surrender</u>.
   d. I'm not going to <u>delay</u> this job any longer.

2 Write out the abbreviations in full:
   a. The T.V. programme I like best is on B.B.C., not on I.T.V.
   b. The two most powerful countries in the world are the U.S.A. and the U.S.S.R.
   c. The P.M. is an M.P. and lives at No. 10 Downing St.
   d. I would like to work for the R.S.P.C.A.

3 Pick out the nouns which are used as adjectives:
   a. He was a freedom fighter during the war.
   b. I need some furniture polish.
   c. The climber spent the night in a log cabin.

4 Write sentences using these nouns as adjectives:
   iron   flower   rice   vegetable   steel

5 Give the homophones of:
   mist   die   road   pair   place   rain
   sun   fowl   vain   peel   wood   not
   days   key   hare   red   flew   two

45 Proverbs

What is the meaning of the sentence, 'Don't count your chickens before they're hatched'?

Can you explain the meaning of the second sentence in this picture?

Proverbs are well-known sayings. The pictures above illustrate two proverbs. Do you understand the meaning of each proverb below?

a. Mrs Brown: You've managed to get some bread. When I went, all the shops had sold out.

   Mrs Black: Ah! *The early bird catches the worm.*

b. James: Joe has been buying sweets for everyone every day this week. Now he's got no money.

   Father: *A fool and his money are soon parted.*

c. Sam: My mum nearly won £100 in a competition.

   Dan: *A miss is as good as a mile.*

d. Louise: The strap on my bag has broken. It's useless now. I wish I'd had it repaired weeks ago.

   Janet: *A stitch in time saves nine.*

Starters

Complete these proverbs:
- a. A bird in the hand _____
- b. One good turn _____
- c. Look before _____
- d. Great minds _____
- e. When the cat's away _____
- f. All's well that _____
- g. More haste _____
- h. New brooms _____

Written Practice

1 Read the sentences below. Then complete the proverbs:
- a. To continue quarrelling makes matters worse.
  Least said _____ .
- b. Too many helpers get in each other's way.
  Too many _____ .
- c. It is best to be honest.
  Honesty is _____ .
- d. Make the most of your opportunities while you can.
  Make hay _____ .
- e. People who have nothing of value to say often talk most.
  Empty vessels _____ .
- f. People with similar ideas and tastes mix together.
  Birds of a feather _____ .
- g. When everything is peaceful, don't stir up trouble.
  Let sleeping dogs _____ .
- h. Changing jobs frequently will not make you rich.
  A rolling stone _____ .

2 Write the proverbs which use these sets of words:
- a. actions louder words
- b. apple day doctor
- c. bird hand bush
- d. fool money parted
- e. friend need indeed
- f. bitten shy
- g. dog day
- h. first served

Free for All

Answer these questions:
- a. What do still waters do?
- b. What begins at home?
- c. What does practice do?
- d. What goes before a fall?
- e. When do the mice play?
- f. Where is there a way?

46 Thesaurus

In 1805 Peter Mark Roget began to compile a catalogue of words which were classed together in sections. Under each topic there are many words associated with each other. The book was published in 1852 and is entitled *Thesaurus*, a treasury of words.

Associated Words

In *Thesaurus* you will find the following words and ideas listed under the word **fear**:
> healthy fear, dread, awe, respect, abject fear, cowardice, fright, stage-fright, affright, funk, wind up, terror, mortal terror, trepidation, alarm, scare, stampede, panic, flight, horror, hair on end, cold sweat, consternation, dismay, hopelessness.

If you look up the word **ship** in *Thesaurus* you will find about two hundred words and phrases associated with ships.

Thesaurus is not a dictionary. It does not give the meanings of words, but words and phrases associated with one idea. Here is how to use it:
> 1 Use the index and find the word or idea you want.
> 2 Turn to the section reference given in the index (**ships** is 275).

Look for a copy of *Thesaurus* in the library, look in the index and find the reference for these words. Then read the words associated with:
> **size   selfishness   action**

Starters

Before using *Thesaurus* again, make three lists of associated words. Think of as many as you can. Start like this:
> **bang tap rap knock shot**
> **street road pavement car lorry**
> **train express passenger goods coach**

When you have written your lists, look up **bang, street** and **train** in *Thesaurus*.

Written Practice

1 From each set write out three words which are most closely associated with each other:
   a. arm wrist ankle head elbow
   b. policeman school traffic pupil teacher
   c. noun verb sentence passage pronoun
   d. plate knife handle blade whistle
   e. dog newspaper television cat radio

2 From each set write out two words that are associated with the first word:
   a. **tree** field trunk leaves gate
   b. **book** page door step chapter
   c. **voice** listen sing silent whisper
   d. **telephone** coin stamp receiver dial
   e. **potato** pan crisps chips fish

2 Make a list of words associated with a supermarket.

4 Make lists of twenty words you associate with:
      motor car   aeroplane   ship

5 Choose one of these hobbies and write out all the words you associate with it:
      football   skating   horse   riding   fishing   painting

47 Where To Look

You cannot know everything, but you should know where to find information:

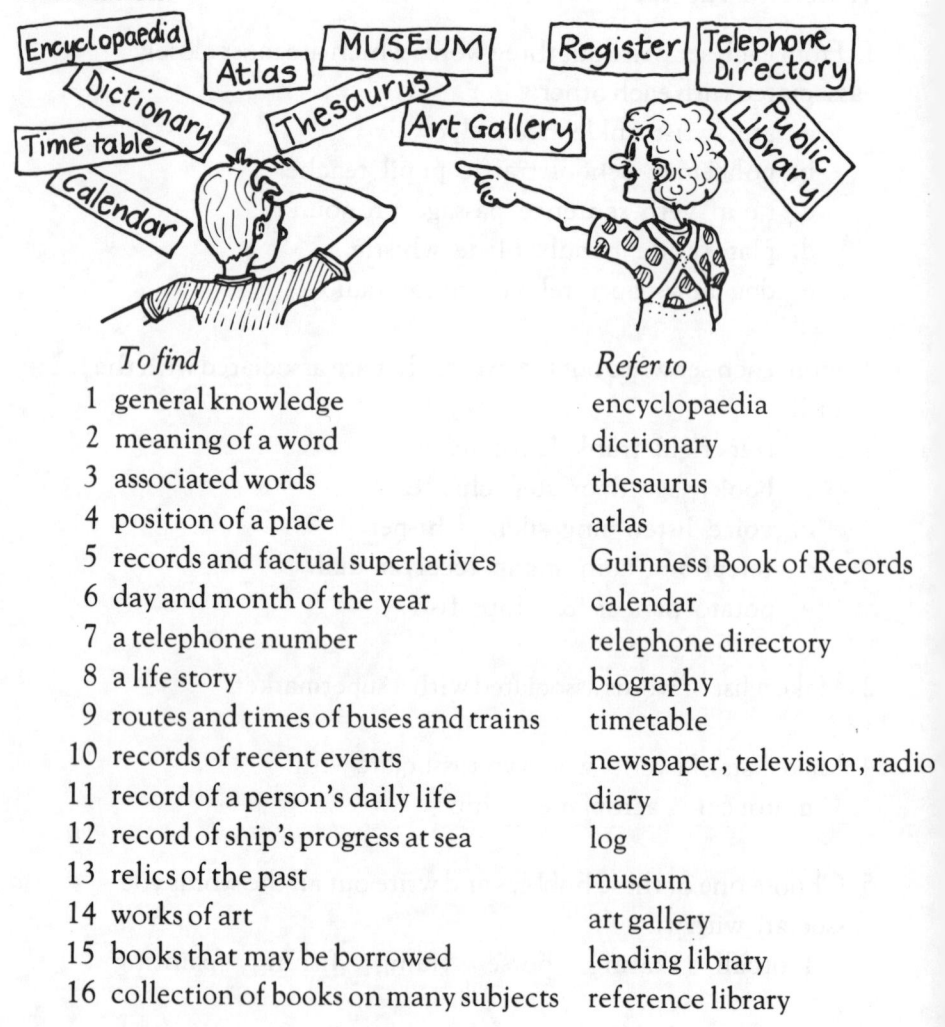

To find	Refer to
1 general knowledge	encyclopaedia
2 meaning of a word	dictionary
3 associated words	thesaurus
4 position of a place	atlas
5 records and factual superlatives	Guinness Book of Records
6 day and month of the year	calendar
7 a telephone number	telephone directory
8 a life story	biography
9 routes and times of buses and trains	timetable
10 records of recent events	newspaper, television, radio
11 record of a person's daily life	diary
12 record of ship's progress at sea	log
13 relics of the past	museum
14 works of art	art gallery
15 books that may be borrowed	lending library
16 collection of books on many subjects	reference library

When you know where to look for information, the important thing is to know how to use the book you refer to. There are three ways you can do it:

1 look at the contents page, usually at the front of a book;
2 look in the index at the back of the book;
3 know how to find what you want in a list arranged in alphabetical order.

Starters

1 This book has a contents page. Find the pages which deal with *gender, homophones, verbs, opposites* and *pronouns*.
2 In the index find the pages which deal with spelling.
3 In a dictionary, look up the meanings of: stale stroll stack steal set

Written Practice

1 Write the meaning of the following words:
   sincere revive essential optimist moderate

2 Explain how you would find information on reptiles in an encyclopaedia.

3 On which day of the week does Christmas Day fall this year?

4 In a library, books are often classified into *fiction* and *non fiction*. In which section of a library would you look for:
   a. a novel
   b. a science book
   c. a 'travel' book
   d. an autobiography
   e. a science fiction book

5 Refer to suitable books and answer these questions:
   a. In which range of mountains is Mount Everest?
   b. Who at present holds the world high jump record?
   c. What are the names of the states of Australia?
   d. What is the address and telephone number of your school?
   e. How many trains a day are there from London to Penzance?

Free for All

1 Find the exchange and telephone number of your nearest:
   library swimming pool cinema
2 From an atlas find which countries these town are in:
   Rome Ottawa San Francisco Peking Moscow
3 Find out which telephone number you dial for:
   the speaking clock a story on the phone the weather forecast

Last Checkpoints

A

1 What are the adjectives made from these nouns?
   health generosity pain strength
   silence England curiosity Holland

2 What are the names of people who sell?
   a. fruit and vegetables
   b. bread and cakes
   c. cod, herring and mackerel
   d. magazines and newspapers
   e. flowers, bouquets and wreaths

3 Write one adverb in place of the words underlined:
   a. I met my friend <u>on this spot.</u>
   b. I must go <u>without waiting any more.</u>
   c. He walked <u>at a fairly rapid pace.</u>
   d. I shall have to leave <u>in a short time.</u>

4 Complete the sentences with these prepositions:
   beside   into   besides   in
   a. The teacher was ____ the classroom.
   b. The teacher walked ____ the classroom.
   c. Jill sat ____ me at the concert.
   d. There were three other girls ____ Jill in our row.

5 Use *you* and *I* or *you* and *me* to complete these sentences:
   a. Tomorrow ____ and ____ will go for a picnic.
   b. ____ and ____ will share this cake.
   c. I shall divide it between ____ and ____.
   d. This is a secret between ____ and ____.

B

1 Complete the second sentence in each pair using a possessive pronoun:
    a. Does this coat belong to you? Is this coat ____?
    b. These things belong to us. These things are ____.
    c. These are your gloves. I am wearing ____.

2 Use a suitable conjunction to complete the sentences:
    a. We waited in the shelter ____ the rain stopped.
    b. Father cooked the dinner ____ mother cleaned the car.
    c. You needn't come to the concert ____ you want to.
    d. The sports were cancelled ____ of heavy rain.

3 Write the following with capitals and punctuation marks:
    how far is it to london asked dick not very far said the stranger with a smile its a fine day for a walk isnt it

4 There are three words which rhyme in each line. Which are they?
    a. blue blow flew slow through
    b. pie pipe sky tight high
    c. deer rode toad stag explode

5 Complete these similes:
    a. as white ____
    b. as black ____
    c. as strong ____
    d. as keen ____
    e. as thick ____
    f. as brown ____

Reference Section

In the following pages you will find information and lists of examples of many items of spoken and written language.

Look here for:
Gender (of people, of creatures)	107
Creatures and their young	108
Collective Nouns (people, animals, other)	109
Idioms	110
Opposites (using different words, adding a prefix or a suffix)	112
Synonyms	114
Prefixes	115
Suffixes	116
Similes	117
Homonyms	118
Making new verbs	119
Abbreviations	120
Compound words	122
Combining words	123
Homophones	124
Proverbs	125
Index	126

Gender of People

Masculine	Feminine	Masculine	Feminine
actor	actress	lord	lady
baron	baroness	male	female
boy	girl	man	woman
bridegroom	bride	master	mistress
brother	sister	Mr	Mrs
brother-in-law	sister-in-law	nephew	niece
count	countess	peer	peeress
duke	duchess	prince	princess
earl	countess	rajah	ranee
father	mother	sculptor	sculptress
father-in-law	mother-in-law	sir	madam
gentleman	lady	son	daughter
grandfather	grandmother	son-in-law	daughter-in-law
headmaster	headmistress	stepfather	stepmother
hero	heroine	steward	stewardess
husband	wife	uncle	aunt
king	queen	widower	widow
landlord	landlady	wizard	witch

Gender of Creatures

Creature	Masculine	Feminine
cat	tom-cat	queen
cattle	bull	cow
deer	buck, hart, stag	doe, hind
duck	drake	duck
elephant	bull	cow
fox	dog-fox	vixen
fowls and birds	cock	hen
goat	billy-goat	nanny-goat
hare	buck	doe
horse	stallion	mare
pig	boar	sow
rabbit	buck	doe
sheep	ram	ewe
swan	cob	pen

Creatures and their Young

Creature	Young	Creature	Young
bear, fox, wolf	cub	goose	gosling
bird	nestling	hare	leveret
cat	kitten	horse	foal, colt, filly
deer	fawn	owl	owlet
dog	pup	pig	piglet
duck	duckling	seal, whale	calf, cub
frog, toad	tadpole	sheep	lamb
goat	kid	swan	cygnet

Collective Nouns

People

an army of soldiers
an audience of listeners
a band of robbers
a bench of magistrates
a choir of singers
a company of actors
a crowd of spectators
a crew of sailors
a gang (of thieves, labourers, youths)
a team (of footballers, cricketers)
a troop of soldiers

Animals

a brood of chickens
a covey of grouse
a drove of cattle
a flock (of birds, sheep)
a gaggle of geese
a herd (of cattle, buffalo, deer, elephants)
a litter (of cubs, pups, pigs)
a pack of wolves
a plague of locusts
a pride of lions
a school of whales
a shoal of herring
a team of oxen

Others

a bouquet of flowers
a bunch (of grapes, bananas, flowers)
a cluster of diamonds
a convoy of ships
a flight (of aeroplanes, steps)
a forest of trees
a library of books
a pack (of cards, lies)
a peal of bells
a skein of wool
a suit of clothes
a set (of spanners, golf clubs, finger-prints, china, drinking glasses)

Idioms

Idiom	Meaning
apple of your eye	someone you especially love
bark up the wrong tree	have a mistaken idea
beat about the bush	not say clearly what one is thinking
beside himself	angry
born with a silver spoon in your mouth	have money and luck from birth
break fresh ground	make new discoveries
break the ice	make a friendly overture
burn your fingers	take a risk and lose
break the back of	do most (or the worst part) of a task
bury the hatchet	make peace
call a spade a spade	speak bluntly
catch red-handed	catch in the act of doing something
catch your eye	attract your attention by looking at you
(a) cold fish	an unfeeling person
cut off your nose to spite your face	do something to your own disadvantage
dead beat	exhausted
down in the mouth	low in spirits
eat out of your hand	be ready to do whatever you want
find your feet	become used to new surroundings
get cold feet	lose courage
get out of hand	get out of control
give the cold shoulder	snub or ignore
give someone his head	allow someone to do as he likes
going flat out	at full speed
good for nothing	useless
have a hand in	have a share in (doing something)
have no leg to stand on	have no reason or excuse
have something hanging over your head	feel a threat
have the last laugh	win at the end, after losing earlier
have your head in the clouds	not paying attention
have your heart in your mouth	be very frightened
hit the nail on the head	do or say something exactly right
in bad shape	in poor health
in hot water	in trouble

in the same boat	in the same circumstances
keep something dark	keep secret or hidden
keep your hand in	practise
laugh in your face	be rude
laugh up your sleeve	laugh secretly
lead up the garden path	deliberately mislead, deceive
leave no stone unturned	investigate thoroughly
let the cat out of the bag	give away a secret
long in the tooth	old, experienced
lose your head	act wildly
make a clean breast of	confess
make a mountain out of a mole hill	exaggerate
nip in the bud	stop at an early stage
no laughing matter	something serious
not as black as you are painted	not as bad as people say you are
on its last legs	very tired, close to death
on tenterhooks	very anxious
over the moon	excited and delighted
playing with fire	risking serious trouble
put your best foot forward	try as hard as possible
put your heads together	think out a plan with others
rub the wrong way	irritate
show a clean pair of heels	run away and escape
sit on the fence	avoid taking sides
smell a rat	feel that something is wrong
(sort out) the sheep from the goats	tell the good from the bad
stand on your own feet	not depend on others
take the bull by the horns	act boldly in spite of risks
thick headed	stupid
throw cold water on	discourage
throw dust in (his) eyes	deceive
throw your hand in	give up
turn over a new leaf	make a fresh start
unable to make head or tail	unable to understand
wash your hands of	refuse to have anything to do with
(a) wet blanket	a discouraging person
wolf in sheep's clothing	a dangerous person who appears harmless

Opposites

1 Opposites by using a different word:

absence	presence	love	hate
alive	dead	more	less
black	white	none	all
buy	sell	north	south
cheap	expensive	often	seldom
clean	dirty	opaque	transparent
difficult	easy	permanent	temporary
divide	multiply	plural	singular
empty	full	quick	slow
entrance	exit	quiet	noisy
everywhere	nowhere	retreat	advance
failure	success	rise	fall
familiar	strange	safety	danger
go	come	solid	liquid
grow	wither	tame	wild
height	depth	true	false
here	there	ugly	beautiful
in	out	unite	separate
innocent	guilty	vague	definite
join	sever	war	peace
junior	senior	wax	wane
kindness	cruelty	young	old
last	first	youth	age

2 Opposites by adding a prefix:

a. prefix *un*

unable	unjust	unhappy	unknown	unpleasant
unsafe	uncommon	unkind	unselfish	unlock

b. prefix *in*

| incapable | inaccurate | infamous | inconvenient | insane |
| inhuman | incorrect | injustice | invisible | indirect |

c. prefix *dis*

| disadvantage | disapproval | disconnect | dishonest | dislike |
| disloyal | disobey | disorder | displeasure | distrust |

d. prefix *im*

| impatient | imperfect | impossible | improper | impure |
| immortal | immoral | immodest | immature | impolite |

e. other prefixes – *ab, ig, il, non, super*

abnormal   ignoble   illegal   nonsense   superman

3 Opposites by changing the prefix:

ascend	descend	external	internal
encourage	discourage	increase	decrease
export	import	inside	outside
exterior	interior	subsonic	supersonic

4 Opposites by changing the suffix:

careful	careless	cheerful	cheerless
hopeful	hopeless	joyful	joyless
merciful	merciless	pitiful	pitiless
useful	useless		

Synonyms

abominable	detestable	keep	retain
accurate	precise	liberty	freedom
avaricious	greedy	maximum	most
baffling	bewildering	minimum	least
banquet	feast	mimic	copy
bounce	rebound	necessity	need
caution	warning	nimble	agile
celebrated	famous	nomad	wanderer
change	alter	observe	watch
demonstrate	show	odour	smell
diminutive	tiny	option	choice
dusk	twilight	prohibit	forbid
enemy	foe	quake	shake
exhibit	show	quit	leave
fatigue	weariness	retreat	withdraw
feeble	weak	saturate	soak
fortify	strengthen	select	choose
fracture	break	terror	fear
gather	collect	transform	change
grab	seize	transparent	clear
gravely	seriously	ultimate	last
hamper	hinder	upright	erect
halt	stop	vacant	empty
hoax	trick	valour	courage
humid	damp	vault	leap
immense	vast	weary	tired
impertinent	insolent	weird	strange
interior	inside	wring	squeeze
jest	joke	yearly	annually
just	fair	yearning	longing

Prefixes

Prefix	Meaning	Examples
a	on	aboard, afloat, ashore
a, ab, abs	away, from	avert, abdicate, absent
ad, ac	to	admit, accept, accede
ante	before	antecedent, anteroom
anti	opposite, against	antibiotic, antidote
bi, bis	two, twice	bicycle, bigamy, biscuit
circum	round	circumference, circumvent
con, com	together	connect, compete, convene
contra	against	contradict, contrary
de	down	descend, depress, decline
dis	away, not	discharge, disappear, disagree
ex	a) out of	extract, export, excursion
	b) formerly, before	ex-Prime Minister
fore	previous	forecast, foretell, foresee
im, in	a) in, into	import, incision, include
	b) not	immovable, impractical, incapable, incorrect
inter	between	international, interval, intervene
mis	wrong, wrongly	misconduct, mischief, misbehave
ob	a) open, clear	obvious, observe
	b) against	obstruct, object, obstacle
post	after	postpone, postscript, post meridian (afternoon)
pre	before	precaution, prepare, preface
pro	a) in front of	proceed, progress, propeller
	b) in favour of	profess, prophet, propose
re	a) again	reappear, retake, repeat
	b) back	return, retrace, rebate
sub	under	submarine, subway, subsonic
super	over, beyond	superior, superhuman
trans	across	transfer, transport, transatlantic
un	not	unimportant, unsafe, untrue
vice	acting for	vice-captain, vice-admiral, viceroy

Suffixes

Suffix	Meaning	Examples
able, ible	capable of being	eatable, edible, recognisable
ian, an	connected with	parliamentarian, publican, magician
ance, ence	state of	remembrance, resemblance, existence
ant	one who	assistant, servant, descendant
et, ette	little	casket, owlet, cigarette
er, eer, ier	one who	joiner, engineer, carrier
ess	female	mistress, princess, waitress
ful	full of	plentiful, meaningful, beautiful
hood	state of being	childhood, knighthood, falsehood
fy	to make	beautify, purify, simplify
less	without	careless, hopeless, meaningless
ling	little	codling, gosling, yearling
ment	state of	contentment, enjoyment, resentment
ock	little	hillock, tussock
ory	a place for	dormitory, factory, priory
ous	full of	courageous, famous, glorious

Similes

as agile as a monkey
as black as night
as black as soot
as blind as a bat
as bold as brass
as brave as a lion
as busy as a bee
as clear as crystal
as cold as ice
as cool as a cucumber
as cunning as a fox
as deaf as a door post
as dry as a bone
as dull as ditchwater
as easy as pie
as fit as a fiddle
as flat as a flounder
as fresh as a daisy
as frisky as a lamb
as gentle as a dove
as good as gold
as graceful as a swan
as green as grass
as happy as a lark
as hard as rock
as hard as nails
as keen as mustard
as large as life

as light as a feather
as mad as a hatter
as obstinate as a mule
as old as the hills
as pale as death
as playful as a kitten
as plump as a partridge
as pretty as a picture
as proud as a peacock
as quiet as a mouse
as red as a turkey-cock
as regular as clockwork
as sharp as a razor
as silent as the grave
as slippery as an eel
as slow as a thrtoise
as smooth as glass
as sound as a bell
as steady as a rock
as strong as an ox
as stubborn as a mule
as sure-footed as a goat
as swift as a deer
as timid as a rabbit
as warm as toast
as wise as an owl
as white as snow
as ugly as sin

Homonyms

(Words which are spelt the same but have different meanings.)

ace (1) one in cards (2) skilled airman
arm (1) limb (2) weapon
bear (1) animal (2) to carry
bank (1) edge of river (2) place to save or borrow money
bark (1) outer cover (2) dog's cry
base (1) low (2) foundation
bat (1) mammal (2) instrument used in cricket
cast (1) throw (2) a mould
catch (1) seize (2) trick
clip (1) fastener (2) cut
club (1) stick (2) place where people meet
dear (1) loved (2) expensive
dock (1) weed (2) place for ships
down (1) lower (2) soft feathers
drill (1) a furrow (2) machine for boring holes
exact (1) precise (2) enforce payment
fan (1) move air (2) keen follower (slang)
fine (1) sum of money (2) of high quality
grave (1) burial hole in earth (2) important
hatch (1) doorway (2) emerge from egg
implement (1) equipment (2) carry out
jam (1) squeeze together (2) a preserve
kind (1) sort (2) gentle
lie (1) falsehood (2) to be at rest
line (1) cord (2) long narrow mark
match (1) contest (2) for lighting a fire
mount (1) mountain (2) climb
nut (1) kernel of a shell (2) metal screw for a bolt
order (1) command (2) arrange in place
peak (1) mountain top (2) brim of a cap
pole (1) shaft of wood (2) north and south
reel (1) sway, stagger (2) cylinder for cotton (3) a dance
rock (1) stone (2) move to and fro
rush (1) run at speed (2) water-side plant
saw (1) tool (2) past tense of see
sound (1) noise (2) solid or safe
sink (1) wash basin (2) submerge in water
trip (1) stumble (2) short journey
tumbler (1) acrobat (2) drinking glass
utter (1) speak (2) total, complete
vice (1) evil (2) tool on bench
wage (1) money for work (2) carry on a war
watch (1) timepiece (2) to look at
wave (1) swell of water (2) movement of hand
yard (1) enclosed ground (2) unit of length
zip (1) fastener (2) energy

New Verbs Made by Adding an Adverb

New Verb	Meaning
catch (someone) out	trick
catch up with	draw level with
draw up (a plan)	arrange
fall out with (someone)	quarrel
get across (an idea)	make it clear
get along	go
get along with (someone)	be friendly with
get away with	succeed in cheating
get off (a letter)	send
get off (with a warning)	escape punishment
get on (in life)	to succeed
get out (of prison)	leave
give away (a secret)	tell
give in (to someone)	surrender, yield
give out (programmes)	distribute
let down (a friend)	fail to keep a promise
let off (a firework)	to cause to explode
make up (a story)	invent
pull through (an illness)	regain health
put about (a rumour)	spread
put off (an idea)	delay
put in for	apply for, make a request
put on (an act)	pretend
put on (speed)	increase
put out by	upset by
run out of (food)	have no more
set out (on a journey)	start
step out	start walking quickly
take up (a hobby)	begin
throw off (a cold)	recover from

Abbreviations

1 Abbreviations used to show a person's rank or title

Mr	Mister	Gen	General
Mrs	Mistress	H.M.	Her/His Majesty
Ms	a married or unmarried woman	H.R.H.	Her/His Royal Highness
Messrs	plural of Mr	Lt	Lieutenant
Capt	Captain	P.C.	Police Constable
Col	Colonel	P.M.	Prime Minister
Dr	Doctor	Prof	Professor
Esq	Esquire	Rev	Reverend

2 Abbreviations used to show a person's qualifications (placed after the name)

B.A.	Bachelor of Arts	M.A.	Master of Arts
B.Mus.	Bachelor of Music	M.D.	Doctor of Medicine
B.Sc.	Bachelor of Science	M.P.	Member of Parliament
J.P.	Justice of the Peace	Q.C.	Queen's Counsel (K.C. King's Counsel)

3 Abbreviations of organisations

A.A.	Automobile Association, Alcoholics Anonymous	N.C.B.	National Coal Board
A.A.A.	Amateur Athletic Association	N.S.P.C.C.	National Society for the Prevention of Cruelty to Children
B.B.C.	British Broadcasting Corporation	R.A.C.	Royal Automobile Club
		R.A.F.	Royal Air Force
B.P.	British Petroleum	R.N.	Royal Navy
B.R.	British Rail	R.N.L.I.	Royal National Lifeboat Institution
C.I.D.	Criminal Investigation Department	R.S.P.C.A.	Royal Society for the Prevention of Cruelty to Animals
Co.	Company		
E.E.C.	European Economic Community	T.U.C.	Trades Union Congress
F.A.	Football Association	Y.H.A.	Youth Hostels Association
I.T.V.	Independent Television		
N.A.T.O.	North Atlantic Treaty Organisation		

4 Other common abbreviations

A.D.	Anno Domini (year of our Lord)	No.	number
a.m.	ante meridiem (before noon)	p.a.	per annum (by the year)
		P.A.Y.E.	Pay As You Earn (Income Tax)
Ave	Avenue	p.m.	post meridiem (afternoon)
b	born		
B.C.	Before Christ	p.c.	postcard, per cent (in each hundred)
B.S.T.	British Summer Time		
c	centigrade, celsius	Pl	Place
C of E	Church of England	P.O.	Post Office, postal order
C.O.D.	cash on delivery	P.S.	post scriptum (written after)
c/o	care of		
Cres	Crescent	P.T.O.	please turn over
Dept	department	R.C.	Roman Catholic
etc	et cetera (and other things)	Rd	Road
		R.S.V.P.	Répondez, s'il vous plaît (reply if you please)
F	Fahrenheit		
h.p.	hire purchase, horse power	S.R.N.	State Registered Nurse
		St	Street
i.e.	id est (that is)	Sq	Square
I.O.U.	I owe you	U.K.	United Kingdom
k.p.h.	kilometres per hour	U.S.A.	United States of America
l.c.m.	least commom multiple	U.S.S.R.	Union of Soviet Socialist Republics
M.C.	Master of Ceremonies, Military Cross		
		v	versus
N.B.	Nota bene (note well)	m.p.h.	miles per hour

Contractions

bike	bicycle	phone	telephone
car	motor car	photo	photograph
bus	omnibus	plane	aeroplane
exam	examination	prom	promenade
gym	gymnasium	vet	veterinary surgeon

Compound Words

1 Two words joined together

bedroom	fireman	knitwear	playground
crossword	flashlight	lampshade	schoolmaster
dartboard	football	lighthouse	skateboard
earthquake	greengrocer	lipstick	spotlight
farmhouse	homwork	manhole	tablecloth
fingerprint	housewife	matchbox	

2 Two words joined with a hyphen

by-product	high-class	know-all	man-made
dry-clean	high-flying	long-range	self-service
flat-footed	hitch-hike	low-lying	skin-tight
hard-hearted	hot-blooded	make-up	spin-off

3 Two separate words used together as a noun

crash barrier	fog horn	living room	swimming bath
cricket bat	ground floor	show jumping	tape measure
Easter egg	ice cream	skimmed milk	tape recorder

Combining Words

Words that can be combined with others to give a special meaning.

Combining Word	Meaning	Examples
-proof	to give protection against	waterproof, fireproof, soundproof, bulletproof, foolproof
-free	without	carefree, dust free, germ free, trouble free, fat free (diet), salt free (diet), tax free

-mate	friend or fellow worker	playmate, schoolmate, workmate, shipmate, helpmate
-power	force	manpower, horsepower
-time		playtime, teatime, springtime, bedtime
-handed		right-handed, left-handed, single handed, one handed, double handed, heavy handed
-shape		heart-shaped, star-shaped, pear-shaped, kidney-shaped
-wise	in the manner of	crab-wise, crosswise, clockwise, lengthwise
-sized		man-sized, giant-sized, king-sized, good-sized (crowd), large-sized (packet)
self-		self-starting, self-propelled, self-taught, self-centred
cross-	across	crossroads, cross-stitch, crossbar, cross-current, cross-wind, cross purposes (opposed), cross examine
fore-	placed at the front	foreword (in a book), forehead, foremost, forefinger, forename, foreman
	before or earlier	forenoon, foresee, foretell, forecast

Homophones

Words having the same sound but different meanings.

air, heir	heard, herd	right, write
allowed, aloud	hole, whole	ring, wring
altar, alter	hour, our	road, rode, rowed
ascent, assent	key, quay	rose, rows
bare, bear	knew, new	sail, sale
beach, beech	knight, night	scene, seen
blew, blue	knot, not	sea, see
board, bored	know, no	seam, seem
bough, bow	leak, leek	sew, so, sow
boy, buoy	loan, lone	sight, site
buy, by, bye	maid, made	soar, sore
ceiling, sealing	mail, male	sole, soul
cellar, seller	meat, meet	son, sun
cereal, serial	medal, meddle	stair, stare
check, cheque	mews, muse	stake, steak
coarse, course	missed, mist	stationary, stationery
council, counsel	more, moor	tail, tale
currant, current	pail, pale	team, teem
draft, draught	pain, pane	their, there
fair, fare	pause, paws	threw, through
feat, feet	peace, piece	tide, tied
flour, flower	peak, peek	too, to, two
foul, fowl	peal, peel	vain, vane, vein
gamble, gambol	peer, pier	waist, waste
groan, grown	plain, plane	wait, weight
hail, hale	practice, practise	week, weak
hair, hare	principal, principle	won, one
hall, haul	rain, reign, rein	wood, would
hear, here	read, reed	you, yew, ewe

Proverbs

(Short, well-known sayings.)
A bird in the hand is worth two in the bush.
A fool and his money are soon parted.
A friend in need is a friend indeed.
An apple a day keeps the doctor away.
A rolling stone gathers no moss.
As well be hanged for a sheep as a lamb.
Birds of a feather flock together.
Cut your coat according to your cloth.
Don't put all your eggs in one basket.
Empty vessels make most noise.
Great minds think alike.
He who pays the piper calls the tune.
Leave well alone.
Let sleeping dogs lie.
Make hay while the sun shines.
More haste, less speed.
New brooms sweep clean.
No news is good news.
No smoke without fire.
Once bitten twice shy.
One good turn deserves another.
Out of the frying pan into the fire.
Still waters run deep.
Least said, soonest mended.
The early bird catches the worm.
Too many cooks spoil the broth.
Two heads are better than one.
Where there's a will there's a way.
When the cat's away the mice will play.

Index

abbreviations 86, 120–121
abstract nouns 47
adjectives 10
    comparing adjectives 44
    showing ownership 10
adverbs 14
    adverbial phrases 14
    comparative adverbs 70
alphabet 4, 38
    alphabetical order 4
    capital letters 4, 26, 36, 50, 60
    vowels and consonants 4
apostrophes
    in shortened words 40
    its and *it's* 40
    showing possession 42

capital letters 4, 26, 36, 50
    summary of use 60
collective nouns 46, 109
common nouns 6
comparative adverbs 70
comparing adjectives 44
compound words 88, 122–3
common words 92
conjunctions 24
    time conjunctions 74
consonants 4
contractions 87
    using apostrophes 40

emphasis 82

gender 16, 107–8

homonyms 80, 118
homophones 94, 124

idioms 58, 110–11
inverted commas 50
its and *it's* 40

link words (who, which, that, whom) 30

metaphors 76

new verbs 84, 119
nouns
    abstract 47
    as adjectives 90
    collective 46, 109
    common 6
    gender 16, 107–8
    proper 26
numbers
    as adjectives 10

opposites 62, 112
ownership 20

plurals
    how to form from different word endings 22
possession 42
possessive pronouns 26
prefixes 62, 68, 112, 115
prepositions 32
pronouns 20
    possessive pronouns 20
proper nouns 26
proverbs 98, 125
punctuation 36, 50

reference books (how to use) 4, 102
related words (different forms of the same word) 28

sentences 36
    capital letters 36
    punctuation 36
singulars 22
similar words 66
similes 72, 117

slang 91
sound patterns 38
spelling 22, 38, 52, 54, 56
suffixes 62, 68, 113, 116
synonyms 114

tenses (past, present, future) 12
thesaurus 100

time conjunctions 74

verbs
  active 8
  making new verbs 84, 119
  passive 8
  tenses 12
vowels 4

Acknowledgements

The author and publishers wish to thank the following who have kindly given permission for the use of copyright material:

Athenium Publishers Inc. for an extract from 'To a Giraffe' published in *Catch Me a Wind* copyright © 1968 by Patricia Hubbell; Curtis Brown Ltd on behalf of the Estate of Kenneth Grahame for an extract from *The Wind in the Willows*; William Heinemann Ltd for the poem 'Slowly' from *The Wandering Moon* by James Reeves; Hodder & Stoughton Children's Books for an extract from *Peter Pan* by J. M. Barrie; Penguin Books for an extract from 'Swarthy smoke-blackened smiths' In Medieval English Verse translated by Brian Stone (Penguin Classics 1964); The Society of Authors as the Literary Representatives of the Estate of John Masefield for an extract from *Cargoes*, and as the Literary Trustees of Walter de la Mare for an extract from *The Fly*; A. P. Watt on behalf of the National Trust of Great Britain for extracts from *The Jungle Book* and *How The Alphabet Was Made* by Rudyard Kipling, and on behalf of the Estate of Sir Henry Newbolt for an extract from *The Highway Man*.

© Edward & Joan Redmayne 1980
Illustrations © Macmillan Education 1980

All rights reserved. No reproduction, copy or transmission of this publication may be made without written permission.

No paragraph of this publication may be reproduced, copied or transmitted save with written permission or in accordance with the provisions of the Copyright, Designs and Patents Act 1988, or under the terms of any licence permitting limited copying issued by the Copyright Licensing Agency, 33–4 Alfred Place, London WC1E 7DP.

Any person who does any unauthorised act in relation to this publication may be liable to criminal prosecution and civil claims for damages.

First published 1980
Reprinted 1987, 1988, 1991

Published by
MACMILLAN EDUCATION LTD
Houndmills, Basingstoke, Hampshire RG21 2XS
and London
Companies and representatives
throughout the world

Printed in Hong Kong

ISBN 0–333–27957–3